# THE GOSPEL OF THE HEART

**Flor McCarthy** is a Salesian priest who has worked as a catechist in second level schools and has extensive parish experience in Ireland and the USA. His other books include *New Sunday and Holy Day Liturgies, Funeral Liturgies* and *Wedding Liturgies*.

*Thanks to the human heart by which we live,*
*Thanks to its tenderness, its joys and fears,*
*To me the meanest flower that blows can give*
*Thoughts that do often lie too deep for tears.*

William Wordsworth

FLOR McCARTHY SDB

# The Gospel
# of the Heart

DOMINICAN PUBLICATIONS

First published (2005) by
Dominican Publications
42 Parnell Square
Dublin 1

ISBN 1-871552-80-X

British Library Cataloguing in Publications Data.
A catalogue record for this book is available
from the British Library.

Cover design by David Cooke

Printed in Ireland by Betaprint Ltd

Acknowledgements
The author and publishers are grateful to those who gave
permission to reproduce copyright material. While every
effort has been made to trace the holder of copyright in texts
quoted, the publishers apologise if any case has been
overlooked, and if an oversight comes to their attention will
make good the omission in any subsequent edition

# Contents

The generous heart
Beatitudes of the heart

Winter in the heart
Springtime in the heart
Gentle and humble of heart
The lightening of burdens
Keeping the heart free of hatred
Getting the heart right
Purifying the heart
Seeing with the heart
Giving with the heart
Receiving with the heart
Working with the heart
Caring for the heart
Healing the wounds of the heart
The heart's memory
The sting
The mercy of fathers

It's the heart That Matters
Witness of Saints, Poets and Philosophers

# Introduction

'IT IS only with the heart that one can see rightly; what is essential is invisible to the eye' (Antoine de Saint Exupery).

Many years have gone by since I first heard those words but I can still remember the impact they made on me. They planted a mustard seed in my imagination which took root immediately. Thanks to its own natural growth, and to a lot of painstaking nurturing on my part, it has now become a fair-sized shrub. To this 'shrub' I have given the title *The Gospel of the Heart*. Drawing its main inspiration from the teaching and example of Jesus, its aim is to show the primacy of the heart in Christian spirituality.

In education we attach more importance to the head than to the heart. Mahatma Gandhi said, 'Western education has stimulated the mind but starved the heart.' In the world of business and politics, many would say that there is no room for the heart. But in spirituality the heart is crucial.

But straightaway a question arises: What do we mean by the 'heart'? Medical people tend to regard the heart as just a pump. Fiction writers tend to depict it as something sentimental, emotional, and romantic. But the Bible sees the heart as the seat of affection, and the centre of our being. In Semitic thought the heart denotes the whole interior life of a human being. It is the part of me where my deepest wisdom and best instincts come from.

The Bible has numerous references to the heart. The most notable of these are included in the book. Our everyday language is liberally sprinkled with references to the heart. The following examples give some idea of the richness contained in the word 'heart'.

When we wish to say that a person is kind, we say that he has *a warm heart*. And when someone is cruel, we say that he has *a cold heart*.

When we wish to describe someone who is exceptionally generous, we say that he has *a heart of gold*.

When we wish to describe a person of impeccable character, we need say no more than that he is a man of *upright heart.*

When someone adopts a stubborn attitude, we say that he is suffering from *hardness of heart.*

When someone has committed himself totally to something, we say that he has put his *whole heart* into it.

When we talk about deep pain, we use the words *heartache* and *heartbreak.*

When someone gives in to despondency, we say that he has *lost heart.*

When we wish to describe the essence of something, we say *the heart of the matter.*

When we feel something deeply, we say that we feel it *in our heart of hearts.*

When we wish to say that we have subjected ourselves to a thorough soul-searching, we say that we have *looked into our heart.*

When we wish to convey that something causes a sense of revulsion within us, we can't put it more forcefully than to say that it makes us *sick at heart.*

When someone has undergone a transformation of character, we say that he has had *a change of heart.*

And disciples of Jesus know that it is by this alone that they will be judged, whether they have loved *with their whole heart.*

There are people who are all head and no heart. This is a sad situation. But the opposite is not ideal either. We must not play down the role of the head. It takes intelligence to use the heart well. The ideal is where head and heart are in harmony. But of the two, the heart is unquestionably the more important, and it is on this that the book concentrates.

A spirituality of the heart is a very down-to-earth spirituality, and also a very joyful one. But that doesn't mean it is an easy one. It is the way of love. Love is the most beautiful force in the world, but also the most demanding.

*Flor McCarthy*

PART ONE

# Taking the Way
# of the Heart

# Growing in the Shadows

THE Irish countryside is at its prettiest in May. The shrubs and bushes are teeming with blossoms. Come September all these blossoms will have vanished. But in their place will be lots of fruit, though most of it of a very modest kind - haws, sloes, and blackberries. Spring represents the promise; autumn the fulfilment.

The in-between period may not appear very exciting or important. Nothing could be further from the truth. It is then that the real work happens. As the blossoms gradually wither and fall, the fruit begins to form and grow. However, the process is so slow and hidden that it can seem as if nothing is happening. It takes approximately a third of the year for the blossoms to turn into fruit.

❧

Something similar happens in our own lives, and it happened it the life of Jesus. A lot of 'fanfare' surrounded his birth. His conception was announced by an angel, and his birth was marked by the singing of angels. But then what happens? He 'disappears' into a little town in Galilee, Nazareth, and doesn't re-emerge until thirty years later. What happened to him in that in-between period?

The heart of a child is very beautiful. At first there is total openness. This enables the child to receive, but it also renders the child very vulnerable. Terrible hurt can be caused to the heart of a child. When a heart is hurt it will harden just to survive. But then its beautiful contents may be lost for ever. The heart of a child has to be protected, just as a bud needs to be protected until it is ready to open.

As a child Jesus too needed that kind of protection. He got it where most children get it - in the bosom of a family. Of all the influences upon us, the family is the most powerful. Here is where we put down our roots. What we draw in through those roots will nourish or poison us for the rest of our lives.

Mary and Joseph welcomed Jesus into the world in Bethlehem. Even though there was no room for him in the inn, they provided a warm space for him in their hearts. Later they provided a home for him in Nazareth. The kind of atmosphere that prevails in the home is crucial.

This atmosphere is determined, not by the quality of the furnishings, but by the quality of the relationships. By their love for him and for one another, Mary and Joseph provided the kind of atmosphere in which Jesus was able to grow in wisdom and in favour with God and people.

They marvelled at the ease with which he learned, and at the quickness of his memory. Still, there is no reason to believe that they had a clear understanding either of his full identity or his great destiny. Nevertheless, in welcoming him into their lives, and in bringing him up in faith and love, they played their part in helping him to realise his destiny.

Only one incident has come down to us from these hidden years. When Jesus was twelve, Mary and Joseph took him to Jerusalem to celebrate the feast of the Passover. While there he got separated from them. After three days of frantic searching they found him in the Temple. Jesus wasn't really lost. Rather, the incident shows that he was beginning to find himself and to discover his true identity. (Luke 2:41-50).

What was he doing during those years at Nazareth? He was growing, maturing, and ripening. Wheat needs about six months in order to grow and ripen. Human beings need many years. The process of maturation can't be rushed. The profound experiences that shape our character and make us what we are take time. Here again we can learn from nature. Nature doesn't take short-cuts. A fruit that has missed a single stage of its ripening never attains fruition.

People must be willing to serve an apprenticeship. Jesus served a long apprenticeship at Nazareth. Nazareth was an ideal place. He was away from publicity, and so was able to grow quietly in the shadows. There were no pressures on him, and no burden of expectations. The main influences in his life would have been home, school, and synagogue.

We must not think that he was simply marking time, waiting for the day when he would begin his public ministry. No. He was living the present moment to the full. The future is contained in the present. Preparing the future is paying attention to the present. The future will be the blossoming of the present. No part of life is useless. Every experience is valuable because it provides an opportunity for growth.

❦

We should treasure the hidden times in our lives, the times when, away from pressures and from the hustle and the bustle, we can grow quietly like corn in the sun. This growth goes on so slowly and quietly that we don't notice it. It goes on without us. Indeed, sometimes it goes on in spite of us.

The thirty years Jesus spent at Nazareth were of crucial importance to him. They gave him an opportunity to tend the garden of his heart. But all the while the consciousness of his true identity and of a call to a special mission was growing within him.

The day he began his public ministry he didn't suddenly became a different person. Rather, on that day he began to share with others the fruits of what had been sown in precious soil, and tended long and lovingly.

Finally the hour of destiny arrived. At thirty years of age Jesus was ripe. So, at the urging of the Spirit, he left Nazareth.

## Receiving the Spirit

B EFORE embarking on his mission, Jesus presented himself to John the Baptist for baptism (Matthew 3:13-17). Now John's baptism was a summons to repentance, and therefore was for sinners. But Jesus was no sinner. So why did he submit himself to it? It seems that he wanted to identify himself publicly with the kind of people he came to save, namely, sinners. And so he began by joining them where they were.

He was identifying not merely with sinners, but with the poor and the downtrodden, who at that time constituted the overwhelming majority of the population of Palestine. He would become their servant and their hope.

What he did that day at the Jordan was to serve as a model for his public ministry. He would not wait for sinners to come to him. He would seek them out. He would befriend them. He wanted them to know that he hadn't come to judge them, but to save them.

This set him at odds with John. John was a preacher of doom; Jesus was a preacher of good news. For John, the Messiah would be an uncompromising judge. For Jesus, the Messiah would be a saviour. John prophesied the judgement of God; Jesus prophesied the salvation of God.

And their approaches were radically different. John was an ascetic, who lived apart from the people. Jesus mixed with the people, eating and drinking with sinners. John was severe; Jesus was radiantly friendly.

But the baptismal experience was very important for Jesus himself. The words, 'You are my beloved son; with you I am well pleased,' deepened his awareness of his divine sonship, and set the seal of divine approval on his future mission.

And at his baptism the Spirit descended on him. In this way he received power for the mission he was about to begin. The Spirit was not given to him just for a moment; the Spirit remained with him throughout his public ministry.

Jesus was continually guided and strengthened by the Holy Spirit. And so his life was characterised by what St Paul calls 'the fruits of the Spirit'. These include such beautiful things as love, joy, peace, patience, kindness, goodness, faithfulness, gentleness, and self-control. (Galatians 5:22).

Jesus left the Jordan, filled with the Spirit. From that moment on his life changed utterly. At last he had found his true vocation. All his hidden qualities of love and care, which had been growing quietly like wheat in a field, would now manifested themselves and be given full expression.

## Purifying the Heart

After his baptism Jesus was confirmed in the belief that he was being called by God to a special mission. At the prompting of the Holy Spirit, he went into the desert to prepare himself for that mission by prayer and fasting. The forty days he spent there also gave him an opportunity to reflect on the nature of the mission and the methods he should employ. While in the desert he was tempted by the devil. (Matthew 4:1-11).

❧

In the first temptation the devil said to him, 'If you are the Son of God, command these stones and they will turn into bread.' But Jesus rebuffed Satan with the words of Scripture: 'A human being does not live on bread alone, but on every word that comes from the mouth of God.'

This doesn't mean that Jesus wasn't concerned about ordinary hunger. He was. In the course of his ministry he would provide bread for people. For instance, when the people followed him into the desert and had nothing to eat, he fed them with loaves and fishes, and did so with great generosity. (John 6:1-15).

So he wasn't downplaying the importance of food. He was well aware that without food no life is possible, much less a higher form of life. However, food is only the beginning. We eat in order to live, not the other way round. He was making the point that food alone will never fully satisfy a human being. 'To nourish human beings is not the same as to fatten cattle' (Antoine de Saint Exupery).

The day after the miracle in the desert, the people came back looking for more of the same kind of bread. But this time he refused to give it to them, knowing they would be little better off for an extra day's food. Instead he said to them, 'Do not work for food that perishes, but for the food that endures for eternal life, food that the Son of Man will give you' (John 6:27).

If he had continued to give the people more loaves and fishes, he would have made himself very popular - in the short term. But in the long term he would have betrayed them. To give priority to their physical needs would be to diminish them. It would be to treat them as no higher than the beasts.

He didn't come to provide ordinary bread. That can be got in the supermarkets. And every day we see people emerging from supermarkets with trolleys laden with food. But we won't find the food that Jesus was talking about in the supermarkets. Only God can give us this other food. Only God can satisfy our deepest hunger. It was this second hunger that would be the main focus of Jesus' mission. His chief task would be to nourish people's minds and hearts with the bread of God's word.

ॐ

Next the devil took Jesus to the pinnacle of the Temple in Jerusalem, and said to him, 'If you are the Son of God, throw yourself down; for scripture says, "He will give his angels charge of you; they will support you on their hands in case you hurt your foot against a stone."' But Jesus said, 'Scripture also says, "You must not put the Lord your God to the test."'

This was the temptation to do something spectacular in order to elicit faith. From the pinnacle of the temple there was a sheer drop down into the Kedron Valley of over 400 feet. If Jesus made that drop and survived, it would have made him a hero, and compelled people to believe in him.

But the temptation was more subtle than this. The devil was right about two aspects of faith. Faith does involve a leap. But not the kind of leap he was suggesting - that can be left to bungee jumpers. Faith doesn't mean we have all the answers. Here on earth there is no such thing as absolute certainty about spiritual things. In that sense, then, faith can be regarded as a leap into the unknown.

And the devil was right when he implied that faith involves absolute trust in God. But that doesn't mean we should test God by putting our lives needlessly in danger. To test God is the opposite to trusting God.

It was a temptation that would be repeated many times during his public ministry. People demanded signs and wonders before they would believe. But he refused to provide them. And on Calvary we hear an echo of the same temptation in the mockery of the chief priests: 'Let him come down from the cross, and we will believe in him. He puts his trust in God; now let God rescue him' (Matthew 27:42-43).

To give in to those kind of demands would be to cheapen faith. Faith is not magic. The person who asks for proof has not learnt the meaning of faith. Besides, holiness doesn't consist in getting God to do our will; it consists in getting ourselves to do God's will.

In the course of his teaching Jesus would urge people to put their trust in God: 'Look at the birds of the air. They do not sow or reap or gather into barns; yet your heavenly Father feeds them. Are you not worth far more than they?' (Matthew 6:26).

And he would give an example of radical trust through the manner in which he died. In spite of the mockery that was directed at him, the darkness that enveloped Mount Calvary, and the acute sense of abandonment he felt, he would die with these words on his lips: 'Father, into your hands I commend my spirit.'

That is faith at its purest.

❦

Finally the devil took him to the top of a very high mountain from where he showed him all the kingdoms of the world and their splendour. And he said, 'All these I will give you, if you fall at my feet and worship me.' But Jesus said, 'Be gone, Satan! For scripture says, "You must worship the Lord your God and serve him alone."'

This was the temptation to set up a political kingdom, with all the trappings of power and glory. Again it was a temptation that would be repeated during his public ministry. After the miracle of the loaves and fishes the people were so impressed that they wanted to take him by force and make him king. But he escaped into the hills by himself. (John 6:15).

Jesus would speak about a kingdom, and do so with great frequency. In fact, he had come to establish a kingdom. But it would not be a political kingdom, but a spiritual kingdom. And it would not be his own kingdom, but the kingdom of God. This kingdom would not be modelled on worldly kingdoms, as the apostles thought. In worldly kingdoms the rulers lord it over their subjects, and those in high places enjoy honour, power, and glory. In the kingdom of God the greatest are those who serve. (Matthew 20:25-26).

The third temptation was the temptation to replace love with power. Power offers an easy substitute for the hard task of love. It is easier to control people than to love people. But Jesus refused the way of power. He had come, not to rule people, but to serve them. He declared himself the obedient servant of the Father, and committed himself to do his will in all things. And today, two thousand years later, millions of people all over the world give him an allegiance which they would not give to any ruler on earth.

❦

The temptations were not necessarily outward experiences. More than likely the battle was fought in the mind and heart of Jesus. But that doesn't make them any less serious. The most subtle and dangerous attacks are the ones that come from inside us.

But can a good person such as Jesus be tempted like the rest of us? The truth is: the good person who resists temptation knows more about its power than the weakling who submits at the very onset of temptation. Hence, if you want to know what victory over temptation costs, don't ask a sinner; ask a saint.

The devil wanted to undermine Jesus in his faithfulness to the Father and to the mission he had received from the Father. But he didn't succeed. Jesus' victory was not an easy one. It was achieved through prayer, fasting, and obedience to the word of God. And that victory was not the winning of the war, but merely the winning of a battle.

The temptations had a positive effect: they helped him to clarify his mind as to the nature of his mission, and to purify his heart as to his motives for embarking on that mission. The temptations also enabled him to repudiate the various false conceptions of Messiahship current among the Jews at that time.

The desert experience helped him in another way. He grew to love solitude, and made a habit of seeking it at difficult moments in his life. When people and events threatened to engulf him, he would withdraw to a lonely place to recover lost energy, and to nurture the most important thing in his life - his relationship with the Father.

# Beginning his Ministry

It seems that what life intends to be great it first makes small. Things that have integrity and truth always seem to start from humble beginnings. We don't know exactly how Jesus began his ministry but we can safely say that it began in a small way. There was no fanfare, no great public launching. The two main components of his ministry were teaching and healing.

❦

As a teacher he made an immediate impact. Crowds flocked to hear him. His teaching made a deep impression on the people. Why? 'Because, unlike the Scribes (the official teachers), he taught them with authority' (Mark 1:22). Yet he held no official position. So where did his authority come from?

Firstly, it came from the fact that he spoke with his own voice. He didn't justify everything he said by quoting the Bible or some other master. At that time no Scribe ever expressed an opinion of his own. He would always buttress his statement with quotations from the great legal masters of the past. But that only showed lack of authority.

Secondly, it came from the fact that he was talking out of experience. Jesus was not a teacher of a subject like history which can be learnt out of books. He was a spiritual teacher. Spirituality has to be lived before it can be taught effectively. That is what he was doing during the thirty years he spent at Nazareth. There is no authority like the authority of the one who has lived what he is saying. Emerson said, 'Only so much do I know as I have lived. Instantly we know whose words are loaded with life.'

Thirdly, it came from the fact that he had that priceless asset - credibility. Credibility is not something that comes with the job. If it comes at all, it comes with the person. Today there is a terrible scepticism about the words of people in authority. The reason for this lies in the fact that many public figures lack credibility. What is it that damages credibility?

When the speaker himself doesn't believe what he is saying. That which we do not believe we cannot adequately say, no matter how often we repeat the words. Jesus spoke with the conviction of one who passionately believed what he was saying.

A flawed character seriously undermines the credibility of a speaker. Just as we are reluctant to drink vine out of a dirty glass, so we are reluctant to listen to a speaker whose character is flawed. Jesus' character was such that it compelled people to listen.

But the thing that most damages the credibility of a speaker is when the speaker doesn't live according to his own words. People may doubt what we say, but they will believe what we do. This caused Emerson to say, 'Do not say things. What you are stands over you and thunders so loudly that I cannot hear what you say to the contrary.' Jesus was the living embodiment of what he preached. He backed up his words with deeds. Every page of the Gospel bears witness to this.

People were also attracted by his style of teaching. His approach was fresh and original. He didn't speak in abstractions. He used concrete images and colourful metaphors. He was able to raise the most profound religious questions through the means of simple things of every day, so that ordinary people were able to understand.

But what most drew people to him was the content of his teaching. Unlike many teachers who are mere providers of facts, he provided vision, inspiration, and meaning. His teaching enlightened the mind, but it also nourished the spirit and set the heart on fire.

There is an incident in the Gospel which is very revealing in this regard. Once when Jesus was teaching in the Temple in Jerusalem, the Pharisees sent the Temple police to arrest him. However, instead of arresting him, they began to listen to him. The result was that they returned to the Pharisees without him. The reason they gave for not arresting him was: 'No one has ever spoken like this man' (John 7:46). That statement, coming from people who would not have been particularly disposed in his favour, speaks volumes.

❧

But it was above all through his deeds that Jesus' luminous goodness manifested itself. This brings us to the second component of his ministry - healing.

The question of suffering was a big problem in Biblical times. Jesus did not go along with the view that suffering was a punishment from God. Nor did he preach resignation. Suffering was one of the evils he came to fight.

Right from the beginning he established a reputation as a healer. St Mark tells us that 'crowds flocked to him, bringing the sick on stretchers to wherever they heard he was. And wherever he went, to village, town, or farm, they laid the sick in the open spaces, begging him to let them touch even the fringe of his cloak. And all those who touched him were cured' (6:55-56).

He healed illnesses of body, mind and spirit. He brought the physically and mentally sick out of the darkness of pain into the light of well-being. He brought sinners out of the darkness of sin into the light of God's grace and love. He brought outcasts out of the darkness of isolation into the light of community. He liberated people who were held bound by 'demons', and enabled them to live in the joy and freedom of the children of God.

Suffering became an opportunity for him to show what God is like. By the way he gave himself to sick people, he revealed the compassion of God in the face of human suffering.

❦

The light of Jesus was not lit once in Palestine and then extinguished. It continues to shine. His words have echoed down the centuries, bringing light to those in darkness and hope to those in despair. And for two millennia his compassionate deeds have illuminated the world.

When the great Russian writer, Leo Tolstoy, underwent a profound crisis of meaning in mid-life, after a futile search elsewhere, he finally turned to the teachings of Jesus. Later he said, 'There I found the purest and most complete doctrine of life. For two thousand years the lofty and precious teaching of Jesus has exercised an influence over people in a way unequalled by anyone else. A light shone within me and around me, and this light has not abandoned me since.' (*Confession*)

Such has been the impact of Jesus that another great Russian writer, Fyodor Dostoevsky, declared: 'While on earth, we grope almost as though in the dark and, but for the precious image of Christ before us, we would lose our way completely and perish.'

## Calling the First Apostles

DURING the course of our lives we have innumerable meetings with people. Most of these turn out to be of no significance, and are soon forgotten. It is a case of surface meeting surface. You could meet some people every day, but it is like a meeting between strangers. Indeed, some of these meetings throw us back on ourselves poorer than before.

But some meetings turn out to be of great significance, and are remembered for ever. Why is this? Because they are not just meetings; they are *encounters*. An encounter is a strange and wonderful thing. In an encounter all barriers fall down. People open their hearts to one another. Life flows from one to the other. One encounter can cause ripples without end across a person's life.

❦

How did the apostles first meet Jesus? Very simply. One day John and Andrew were standing by the river Jordan with John the Baptist. When the latter saw Jesus passing by he said, 'There he is! He's the one I was telling you about. He's the lamb of God who will take away the sins of the world.'

Here we see the greatness of John the Baptist. He knew that his mission was to prepare the way for Jesus. Hence, when Jesus appeared on the scene, he knew that his task was done. Having introduced Jesus, he stepped aside and allowed Jesus to take over. That took greatness.

Leaving John, the two disciples set off after Jesus. Noticing that he was being followed, Jesus stopped and asked, 'What do you want?'

'Teacher, where do you live?' they asked.

'Come and see,' he said.

Jesus led them to where he was living, and they spent the rest of that day in his company. They didn't have just a meeting with him; they had an encounter with him. That encounter remained so etched in John's memory that years later he was able to recall the exact time of day in which it happened - four o'clock in the afternoon. We don't know what they talked about. But a spiritual affinity was created between them, and a rare friendship was born.

The two disciples were so excited that they wanted to share their joy with their friends. Early next morning Andrew brought his brother, Peter, to meet Jesus. The following day Philip and Nathanael joined them. This little group of five were to form the nucleus of the group that later became known as 'the twelve apostles'. (John 1:35-51).

❦

Those first disciples were clearly captivated by Jesus. But it is also clear that Jesus saw something special in them, because a little later he called them away from their jobs to permanent discipleship. And they left everything - livelihood, possessions, family ties - and followed him.

When the leaders of cults wish to recruit disciples they appeal to people's fears and weaknesses. But that is to manipulate them, and take away their freedom. Jesus did not appeal to the weaknesses of those first disciples. He appealed to their strengths, and had total respect for their freedom. As a consequence their commitment had deeper roots.

Though Jesus did not exercise power over those first disciples, he did exercise influence on them. Those who exercise influence on others do not try to convert them, or change them, or mould them. On the contrary, they offer them the space in which they can find themselves.

Through their contact with Jesus those first disciples began to discover themselves. Because of the kind of person he was, they got a vision of what they themselves might become. An encounter with him was like a voyage into another world.

When Jesus eventually called them to permanent discipleship, he said, 'Follow me and I will make you fishers of people' (Mark 1:18). From this they understood that his call was a call to service of others. The leaders of cults call people to follow them, and then turn them into their personal slaves. Jesus called the apostles, not to the service of himself, but to the service of others.

The apostles also knew that he wasn't calling them to a life of ease. Quite the contrary. But as fishermen they would have been well acquainted with hardship already. They were not afraid of sacrifice.

They realised that his call also held great possibilities for themselves. It provided them with an opportunity to live deeper and more worthwhile lives. Fishing was an important occupation. But Jesus called them to a more important occupation. He offered them not just a new work, but a cause to which to dedicate their lives.

Up to this they had a career. Now they had a vocation. A career and a vocation are different though not mutually exclusive. A vocation might be expressed through a specific career, such as that of teacher or nurse, for example. But a vocation can never be reduced to these activities. It is something deeper. It involves vision, motivation, and dedication. A career usually means furthering oneself. A vocation always means serving others.

There is a tendency to regard the apostles as supermen. They were not supermen. They were just ordinary people. No one ever believed in the ordinary people as much as Jesus did.

## Encountering Bigotry

OF ALL human traits bigotry is probably the most repulsive. Bigotry gives us an insight into the abyss of wickedness that lies hidden in the human heart until conflict releases it. It is particularly repulsive when found in religious people.

In the 1980s the 'Troubles' in Northern Ireland were at their worst. A lot of people were getting killed. David Armstrong, then a Presbyterian minister, didn't think the Churches were doing enough to break down the fear and mistrust that exist between the Protestant and Catholic communities in the North. He said, 'We shouldn't limit our role to that of burying the dead. We must try to bring about a situation where there will be no dead to bury.'

He decided to do something about it. On Christmas morning, 1984, he went across the road to convey Christmas greetings to the local Catholic priest, Kevin Mullan. Kevin Mullan received him warmly and invited him to addressed the parishioners who were still in Church. Because he had no prepared script, David hesitated, but then agreed to do so. He said a few words from the heart about peace and goodwill, and got a tremendous reception.

Later that morning Kevin Mullan went over to David Armstrong with a message for his congregation. David invited him to deliver it personally to the congregation. He did so. And something beautiful was born.

What David Armstrong did that Christmas morning was only a small gesture. Yet it provoked a storm of opposition from Ian Paisley's Free Presbyterian Church. Nothing had prepared him for the level of hostility he encountered. It brought him face to face with hate. His church was picketed by Paisley's supporters, and he and his family received death threats.

Now David is a brave man and a committed Christian. He says, 'You have to do what is right, and take the consequences.' Nevertheless, things became so difficult that for the sake of his family he had to leave the North. The experience toughened him, but it didn't harden or embitter him. He is now ministering as an Anglican priest in the South of Ireland.

David Armstrong is a good man. He set out to make friends, yet ended up making enemies. A similar thing happened to Jesus when he went back to preach to his own people in Nazareth.

❦

Jesus didn't begin his preaching in Nazareth, but in the neighbouring town of Capernaum. After some time there he went back to Nazareth and to the people among whom he had grown up. He wanted to bring them too the benefit of his gifts. On the Sabbath day he went to the synagogue. On entering the synagogue he sensed a coldness in their attitude towards him. Still, they honoured him by inviting him to do the scripture reading, and to give the address.

They handed him the scroll of the prophet Isaiah. Unrolling the scroll he found the passage where it is written: 'The spirit of the Lord has been given to me, for he has anointed me. He sent me to bring good news to the poor, to bind up hearts that are broken, to proclaim liberty to captives, release to those in prison, and to proclaim to all a year of the Lord's favour' (61:1-2).

He rolled up the scroll, gave it back to the attendant, and sat down. Everything was quiet, everything was orderly, as befitted the house of God. The eyes of all were fixed on him. Then he said, 'Today these words are fulfilled in your hearing.'

The people quickly grasped what he was saying: the messianic vision of pardon, healing, and liberation was about to become a reality. They greeted the news with enthusiasm. But when he claimed a central role for himself in bringing this about, their enthusiasm turned into scepticism.

They still saw him as just the son of Joseph, a local carpenter. How could such a one as he fulfil the beautiful words of Isaiah? And yet it seemed that he was capable of great things. In fact, if they could believe what they had heard, he had already done them, but not among them. He had done them in Capernaum. They resented this. If he had something to offer, why didn't he begin with his own people? So they said to him, 'Why don't you do here in Nazareth the kind of things you did at Capernaum?'

His answer was that he couldn't do them because of their lack of faith in him. He did them in Capernaum because he had found people there who had faith in him. This didn't go down well with them. But then he went on to hint at the inclusion of the Gentiles in the messianic blessings, giving two examples of Gentiles who had been helped by two of their greatest prophets, Elijah and Elisha. He reminded them of how Elijah had saved a Sidonian widow and her son during a famine (I Kings 17:7-16), and how Elisha had cured a Syrian general, Naaman, of leprosy (2 Kings 5::1-27).

It was at this point that things turned ugly. As Jews, they despised Gentiles. So, in a burst of nationalistic fervour, they turned on him, and hustled him out of the synagogue. Then they took him to the brow of a hill, intending to throw him over, but he escaped through their midst.

Jesus shared the fate of every true prophet - rejection by his own people. He was saddened that, because of the people's lack of faith, he wasn't able to do for them what he dearly wanted to do. But he didn't get embittered and bury his gifts. He did what he could for the few who believed in him, and then took his gifts elsewhere.

If you have ever wondered how such a transparently good person as Jesus ended up being crucified you need look no further than this incident for the answer. There can be no doubt but that the people of Nazareth really intended to kill him. (It was probably not them all, but merely a bunch of bigoted fanatics). What makes it so shocking is the fact that they did it in the name of religion. (Luke 4:16-30).

❦

Religion is a beautiful thing, but it can get distorted and turn into something repulsive. Religion then becomes synonymous with intolerance, fanaticism, and bigotry.

Religion brings out the worst in some people. It makes them more bigoted, and more apt to hate and kill. But religion brings out the best in other people. It makes them more tolerant and more loving. True religion liberates the heart and the mind, and fosters harmonious relationships with others. Religion is beautiful when it is like this.

There is an essential link between faith and love. We can't worship God if our heart is full of bitterness and hatred. Hatred towards any human being and love of God cannot exist in the same heart.

PART TWO

# *Encounters of the Heart*

# Touching the Untouchable

U SUALLY we can see at a glance people's physical illnesses and disabilities. But what we see may constitute only part of their pain. Sometimes there is a whole other side to it that we cannot see, at least not immediately.

Once I was chatting to a man in a nursing home. His physical problem was immediately obvious to me – he was missing both legs. He told me that some months prior to this he had to have his legs amputated because of gangrene. Up to that time he had been running his own farm, and was busy from dawn to dusk. Now he was completely idle, and spent the day sitting in a wheelchair, looking out the window. I tried to imagine how he felt. But I had to hear it from himself. And I did. At a certain point he said to me, 'I'm nearly gone insane trying to pass the time.'

❧

One day a man approached Jesus. Jesus saw at a glance that his body was hideously disfigured by leprosy. At that time no disease was regarded with such terror and pity as leprosy. The disease was bad enough in itself, but the social consequences of it were even worse. Leprosy was considered to be the ultimate uncleanness.

A leper's existence was a cold and lonely one. Lepers were banished from the community, and had to live apart. They were also excluded from the religious life of the people. At that time illness was seen as a consequence of sin. This meant that lepers were also regarded as sinners. As such, it was assumed that God too had cut them off.

Lepers were not supposed to appear in public without giving a warning. It seems this man appeared without giving the required warning. In so doing he was running the risk of being stoned. However, he was so determined to meet Jesus that he was prepared to take that risk.

Now Jesus knew what society thought of lepers. How would he deal with a man who was, in the words of St Luke, 'covered with leprosy'? Would he keep him at a distance? Would he even shun him altogether? Well, as it happened, he did neither. He allowed him to come right up to him.

Then the leper said. 'Sir, if you want to, you can cure me.' Jesus didn't reply immediately. He did something better. He stretched out his hand and touched the leper. Then he said, 'Of course I want to. Be cured.' And all at once the leprosy left him. (Luke 5: 12-16).

❦

'Of course I want to.' These simple words convey warmth and generosity. Jesus didn't see the leper as unclean. He saw him simply as a human being in desperate need. But it is in the gesture of touching the leper that the compassion of Jesus shines out. However, that gesture must have shocked the onlookers. What Jesus did was forbidden by law. Besides, in touching the leper, Jesus had become ritually unclean himself. So why did he do what the Law forbade?

He touched the leper because that's the kind of person he was. In itself it was a small gesture. However, small gestures can give us greater insight into a person's character than big gestures. Big gestures show us a person's power. Small gestures show us a person's humanity. In this small gesture we see Jesus' compassion for the outcast.

He touched the leper because he saw that he needed healing not only in body but also in spirit. His body was horribly wounded by leprosy. But his spirit was deeply wounded as a result of having been rejected by everyone, and seemingly by God too. Jesus healed not only his ravaged body but also his wounded spirit, and thus restored his lost dignity as a human being and a child of God.

He touched the leper so that he might show us that external uncleanness does not defile the clean of heart. He touched the leper to teach us to despise no one, or regard them as pitiable, because of some bodily affliction.

Jesus accepted the leper just as he was. Acceptance is the answer to rejection. It is one of the loveliest things that can happen to anyone. It is the love and acceptance of others that makes us the unique persons that we are, and enables us to realise our full potential.

In order to have the cure authenticated, and thus ease his return to society, Jesus ordered the leper to go and show himself to a priest. He also asked him to keep quiet about his cure. Some chance! The leper broadcast everywhere what Jesus had done for him. No doubt he also spoke about the astonishing kindness and respect with which he had treated him.

❦

This was not a once-off act on Jesus' part. This was his usual way of dealing with the sick, with sinners, and with outcasts. He didn't keep his distance from them. He reached out and touched them. Physical contact is precisely what gives such people a feeling of acceptance. Concern and love are communicated more by touch than by words. For someone in the leper's condition to be touched with love and respect would in itself have been a tremendously healing thing.

The example of Jesus humbles us, because he shows up the poverty of our hearts. While we may be moved to give a little money to a beggar, we make sure there is no physical contact between us, and probably no verbal or eye contact either. But the example of Jesus also challenges us. 'He that by me spreads a wider breast than my own proves the width of my own' (Walt Whitman). If only we could overcome the fear we feel in the presence of the poor and the sick, and reach out to them, we would discover how much we have to give.

Jesus' example also constitutes a powerful challenge to society and especially to the Christian community. Jesus broke through the religious and social taboos of his time, and reached out a loving and healing hand to the leper. The Christian community should follow his example and reach out to the wounded and the excluded.

## Quenching the Deeper Thirst

O F ALL the commodities with which our earth has been blessed water is the most precious. But one has to have some experience of the desert to appreciate just how precious it is. The most basic thing water does for us is to quench our physical thirst. But we have a deeper thirst which ordinary water cannot quench. In his Gospel St John tells of an encounter between two thirsty people, one suffering from physical thirst, the other suffering from a spiritual thirst, and how each quenched the thirst of the other.

One day as Jesus and his apostles were passing through Samaria they came to a well known as Jacob's well. It was noon. Tired from the journey, Jesus sat down by the side of the well, while the apostles went into a nearby town to buy food.

As he sat there in the midday sun, a woman came to draw water. The fact that she came to draw water at noon and alone suggests that she was an outcast from her community. One thing is clear: she was a deeply troubled woman, having suffered no less than five broken marriages.

Jesus treated her with great sensitivity. He didn't confront her about her lifestyle. Had he done so she would surely have clammed up. He could see that she was thirsting to be seen as a person and not as an object. So he adopted a very gentle approach. He began the dialogue from a position of weakness. He began by asking her for a drink of water.

The woman was astonished that a Jewish man would speak to her, let alone ask a favour of her. At that time, a centuries-old feud existed between the Jews and the Samaritans. But thirst is a great leveller. She gave him the water. As she did so she said, 'You must be the first Jewish man in history to ask a Samaritan woman for a drink.'

Jesus drank the water. Grateful for the simple but beautiful gift she had given him, he felt a desire to give her something in return.

So he said to her, 'If only you knew the gift God gives, and who I am, then it is you who would have asked me for a drink. And I wouldn't have given you this stagnant water. I would have given you running water.'

Thinking that he was talking about ordinary water, the woman said, 'Sir, you have no bucket, and the well is deep. So how can you give me water to drink?'

'You know well,' Jesus replied, 'that those who drink this water will get thirsty again. But those who drink the water I can give, will never know thirst again. They will have an eternal spring inside themselves.'

The woman didn't get it. Still thinking that he was talking about ordinary water and ordinary thirst, she said, 'Sir, give me some of that water so that I may never get thirsty, and never have to come here again to draw water.'

Jesus was very patient. The woman sensed his care for her. She didn't feel judged. She felt accepted. Before she realised it, she had shared with him the whole story of her sad life.

Then he explained to her that what she was experiencing was only the deeper thirst which affects everyone, the thirst for God. The psalmist put it like this: 'Like a deer that yearns for running streams, so my soul is yearning for you, my God. My soul is thirsting for God, the God of my life; when can I enter and see the face of God?' (Psalm 42:2-3).

For this deeper thirst we need another kind of 'water'. What is this water? It is the life of God inside us. The discovery of God is like a spring within us.

At a certain point the apostles arrived back, and that was the end of the encounter. The woman was overwhelmed by the kindness and understanding of Jesus. She was so excited about what he had said to her that she left her water jar behind, and ran back into the village. To everyone she met she said, 'Come and see a man who told me the whole story of my life.'

Of course, by 'the whole story' she didn't mean her complete biography. What she was really saying was: 'Here is someone who knows exactly what my life has been like. Here is someone who really understands me.' We may ask how someone as pure as Jesus could understand a woman like her? 'Only the pure of heart forgive the thirst that leads to dead waters' (Kahlil Gibran).

The woman was greatly enriched as a result of her encounter with Jesus. Yet he didn't give her any*thing*. What he did was to awaken her to a sense of the goodness of God, and of her own great dignity as a child of God. (John (4:5-30).

༓

Jesus meets us where we are. He knows that we are always thirsting for something else. To experience this thirst is not a curse but a blessing. It disposes us to receive the 'living water' that Jesus wishes to give us. Ordinary water is a very precious commodity. But the water Jesus gives is more precious still.

## Awakening the Heart

IT'S amazing how seeds can lie dormant for years until the soil is disturbed and some new element is added to it, and then they suddenly blossom.

There is a piece of road in my native County Kerry with which I am very familiar. For years it was a barren, bleak stretch. Now, however, every summer its margins are covered with an array of beautiful flowers. One species stands out - the ox-eye daisy. This little miracle happened because in the process of upgrading the road the margins were dug up and lime from the crushed stone used on the road was added to the soil.

༓

One day, as Jesus was passing through Capernaum, he saw a man called Matthew sitting on the steps in front of the Tax Office. He said to him, 'Follow me.' And Matthew got up at once and followed him. (Matthew 9:9).

༓

Matthew was a surprising choice on Jesus' part. He was a tax collector. At that time tax collectors were hated by the people - they were seen as collaborators with their foreigners occupiers, the Romans. Those who were in the tax-collecting business were in it for themselves.

But even more surprising was Matthew's immediate and whole-hearted response to the call of Jesus. How do we account for this? It can only mean that he was ripe for the call. Conversions are seldom as sudden as they seem. 'No single event can awaken in us a stranger completely unknown to us' (Antoine de Saint Exupery).

But what was it that brought him to this point of 'ripeness'? It may be that he was finding the job of tax collecting soul destroy-ing, which meant he was not a happy man. The saddest and loneliest moments in life are when we are alienated from our-selves, or when we have betrayed our better self. Besides, he was conscious of being hated and despised by his own people. That was no way to spend one's life. He may have been successful, but at what cost?

But these are negative factors. There must have been positive reasons for his decision to leave everything and follow Jesus. He was conscious of a stranger sleeping within him. Deep down inside him was an unfulfilled yearning for goodness. The job of tax collecting was threatening to stifle that yearning. He sensed a hardness developing in himself. However, his heart hadn't yet become like cement. So when Jesus offered him a chance to do something better with his life, he grabbed it immediately and with both hands. And a dream, half dead, suddenly flared into life.

No doubt he was also impressed by the fact that Jesus noticed him. As we know, it's nice to be noticed. But what would have made an even deeper impression on him was the fact that Jesus had read the thoughts of his inmost heart. Here was someone who understood his dreams. Here was someone who had seen into his most intimate and secret longings, longings about which he had never dared speak to anyone. No one else had seen this side of him. Jesus was the first to see those possibilities in him.

Still, the decision to follow Jesus can't have been an easy one for him. In meant turning his back on a secure and lucrative job. It meant sacrificing his own plans and ambitions. It meant being transported from a world of comfort and choice into a wilderness. It meant ceasing to exploit people and setting out to serve them.

But he knew that he was being called to a new and more abundant life. He would have his eyes opened, his ears unplugged, and his heart broken open. Dead parts of himself would be brought to life. His true character would have a chance to emerge and develop. The call of Jesus was like a warm, fructifying sun which shone especially for him, and which in due time would bring all his gifts to blossom and ripeness.

Before his encounter with Jesus, he had lost his bearings. The star he had been following had betrayed him. From now on he would have a star that would not play him false, a compass that would not lie to him.

❦

Today in the western world vocations to the priesthood and the Religious Life have almost completely dried up. The caring professions and voluntary organisations are experiencing a similar drought. Society has become very materialistic and very individualistic. The idea of devoting one's life to a purpose beyond one self is profoundly counter-culture. It is not easy to allow oneself to be chosen when all the emphasis is on the economy, on success, on self.

And yet, there is a fulfilment beyond all this. Far and away the best prize that life has to offer is the chance to work at something that is worth doing and that transcends oneself and one's own interests.

The great thing about Matthew was that he was open to change. He had the courage to answer a call, even though that call subverted all his values. Thus he challenges us. We can become so focused on our own goals and schedules that we refuse to be involved in anything that threatens those goals and schedules. Without realising it, we can create a world in which the ego is king.

The ego is never happier than when controlling the agenda.

Besides, for all our industry, we may be stagnating. Each of us has a greater possibility. In the words of Emerson, 'There is in each of us a chamber, or a closet, that has never been opened.' If we are to realise this greater possibility, we need to be challenged to go beyond what we think we are capable of or have settled for.

All people are capable of bursts of greatness, such as in times of emergency. But when things return to normal they go back to sleep. However, now and again something happens that causes the soul of a particular person to burst into flame, so much so that afterwards he or she is never the same again.

The quality of people's lives is affected, not so much by what is given to them, as by what is asked of them.

## Curing the Whole Person

I T seems incredible that we can have such a strong resistance to what we most deeply desire. For instance, when we go to a doctor, we don't like to be treated in a hasty and impersonal manner. Yet often we are content with a 'quick fix'. Why is this? Because there is a part of us that shies away from a personal encounter. Even though we know that an encounter is more enriching, we also know that it is more demanding. That is why we want to get it over with as quickly as possible.

❧

One day a sick woman came to see Jesus, and a 'quick fix' is exactly what she was looking for. She had been suffering from a haemorrhage for twelve years, and had spent all her money on doctors. But it was money down the drain.

When she heard that Jesus was in the area, she was determined by hook or by crook to meet him. However, she wasn't seeking an encounter with him. All she wanted was to touch the hem of his robe. She was convinced that if she could do that she would be cured.

She was a very determined lady. All around Jesus people were pushing and shoving in an effort to get near him. Yet, in spite of her illness, this woman somehow managed to get through the crowd and up behind him. Then she reached out and touched the hem of his robe, and her bleeding stopped immediately. Now to get away as quickly and quietly as possible. However, just as she was about to slink off into the anonymity of the crowd, Jesus turned to the apostles and asked, 'Did you see anyone touching me?'

'Dozens of people have touched you,' one of them replied,

'Dozens of people have brushed up against me. But this was different. I felt power going out of me,' he said.

He continued to look around him. Finally he spotted her. 'Was it you that touched me?' he asked.

'Yes, Sir,' she replied, trembling.

She had good reason to tremble. A woman with a haemorrhage was consider to be ritually unclean. She had no business in the crowd. By touching Jesus, she had rendered him ritually unclean too. But far from scolding her for her 'reprehensible' conduct, he said, 'Have no fear. Your faith has made you well. Go in peace, my daughter.' (Mark 5:25-34).

❦

Jesus went out of his way to make contact with sick people. He never cured just an illness; he cured a sick person. But all this particular woman wanted from him was a cure for her illness. However, he insisted on meeting her. In this, he was not thinking of himself but of her. He knew she needed not only physical healing but also psychological and spiritual healing. After all her years of sickness she was feeling bad about herself.

During his encounter with her he spoke lovely words to her. By addressing her as 'daughter', he made her understand that she was a child of God and a chosen one. This did far more for her than a hasty, impersonal, and secretive cure.

❦

Some healers reduce human contact to a minimum. They treat a sickness rather than a sick person. Elizabeth Kubler-Ross gives the example of one terminally ill woman literally crying out, 'All my doctor wants to discuss is the size of my liver. At this point, what do I care about the size of my liver. I have five children at home who need to be taken care of. That's what's killing me. And no one will talk to me about that!'

Some doctors are too detached in their approach to their patients. They are not willing to confront patients' fears and defences. So they keep patients at arm's length. It's not that they don't care. They may care deeply, but hide it behind a barrier of professional detachment. Why? Because they are afraid of being overwhelmed by the constant daily contact with suffering. Yet if they knew how their patients feel, they would be able to treat them with more compassion, the same compassion they would want for themselves.

This is why the role of nurses and nurses aides is such a vital one. Primarily they are *carers* rather than *curers*. They have more contact with their patients. In hospitals and nursing homes they do the basic, intimate things – waking, bathing, dressing, feeding, and bedding down for the night. It is their eyes, their voices, their manner and touch that form the texture of daily life for thousands of dependent people.

Dostoevsky had a point when he said that kindness is as important to the patient as medicine. People must *know* themselves cared for. Curing without care may heal a person's physical illness but it won't heal the whole person. If you treat an illness, you will win sometimes and you will lose sometimes. But if you treat the whole person, you will win every time regardless of the outcome.

❦

What did Jesus mean when he said, 'I felt power going out of me'? To achieve success at anything we have to put something of ourselves into it, so much so that we may feel drained afterwards. This is especially true of healing. Every time Jesus healed someone it took something out of him.

Each of us is capable of doing some healing. With a little care we could ease a troubled mind. With a little of our time we could ease the pain of loneliness for someone. With a little sympathy we could heal a wounded heart. But each act of caring will cost us something.

However, sometimes there is nothing we can do for the sufferer, and nothing we can say either. In that case our only ministry is that of simple presence, like that of Mary at the foot of the cross. It is a ministry of powerlessness. Yet, just by being there, by standing alongside, we save the sufferer from feeling abandoned, and offer something very precious, namely, human comfort.

A person can be healed without being cured. Dying patients are never healed in the physical sense, but they can get better emotionally and spiritually. So, while we may not be able to cure, it is within our power to care. And caring is a very healing thing. 'A compassionate heart can heal almost anything' (Elizabeth Kubler-Ross, *The Wheel of Life*).

## Living on the Sunny Side

O N some winter days in Ireland you get a peculiar phenomenon. You get warm sunshine and widespread frost and ice. If you go for a walk out-of-doors, one minute you can be walking in brilliant sunshine, next minute in freezing shade. The world of sunshine makes you feel good to be alive. But the world of freezing shade makes you want to run for cover.

Something similar can happen in the world of people. You can walk into a room filled with people, and it's like walking into sunshine. And you can walk into anotehr room, and it's like walking into a frosty shade.

❦

One Sabbath day Jesus went into a synagogue, and immediately sensed a hostile atmosphere. It was like walking into a freezing shade. Right in front of him they had placed a man with a withered hand. The religious leaders were watching him like hawks to see if he would heal him. If he did, then they could charge with breaking the Sabbath.

But Jesus knew what their game was, and decided to take them on. Turning to the man with the withered hand, he said, 'Step out into the middle.' The man did so willingly. All he wanted was a cure, Sabbath or no Sabbath. Then turning to the religious leaders, Jesus said, 'Tell me. Is it permitted to cure a person on the Sabbath?' But they refused to answer.

'I see,' he said, 'so you won't answer me. Well then, let me ask you another question. Suppose one of you has a sheep, and it falls into a hole on the Sabbath day, would you pull it out?'

Still no reply. Only sour looks. So he answered the question himself. 'Of course you would. Now, if it's permitted to save a sheep on the Sabbath, surely it's permitted to save a human being?'

Then he turned back to the man and said, 'Stretch out your hand.' The man did so and his hand came right. And Jesus said to them all, 'Learn a lesson from this. The Sabbath was made for people, not people for the Sabbath.'

The man went away wrapped in a warm glow of well-being. But the Pharisees were furious, and began to plot how to do away with Jesus. (Matthew 12:9-14).

❦

There are certain people who bring the sunshine with them wherever they go. They exude warmth. Jesus was such a person. Wherever he went he radiated warmth, so that people were drawn to him. However, not everyone was so affected by his presence. There were those who were implacably hostile towards him, and who chose to remain in the cold.

The human heart has its sunny side and its frosty side. To some people we show our sunny side; to others our frosty side. But when we adopt a frosty attitude to someone we are condemning ourselves to the cold also, whereas when we adopt a sunny attitude to someone we are exposing ourselves to the sun also.

## Receiving a Sinner

O NCE, on the eve of an All-Ireland Football Final in Dublin, I was looking for accommodation for a friend. My search took me to the doors of at least two dozen Bed and Breakfasts and small Hotels in and around the centre of the city. In every case I was met with, 'Sorry, but we're full up.' I can tell you that it left me with a very empty feeling.

When the time came for Jesus to be born there was no room in the inn at Bethlehem, so he was born in a stable and laid in a manger. 'There was no room in the inn.' This is one the saddest phrases in the Gospel. And why was there no room in the inn? Because there was no room in the heart of the innkeeper. If we have room for a person in our heart, we will make room for that person in our home.

ॐ

A Pharisee by the name of Simon invited Jesus to his house for a meal. Now at that time it was the custom to do certain things for an honoured guest. As soon as the guest arrived, the host greeted him with a kiss as a sign of welcome. Then he gave him a basin of water to wash his feet. (All the roads at that time were dirt roads). Finally, he poured a little perfume on his head. These were just normal signs of courtesy. Yet, for some reason, Simon didn't give any of them to Jesus. So Jesus sat down to the meal just as he was.

Now during the meal a woman who had a bad name in the town entered the room and knelt down at the feet of Jesus. Of course, she had no right to show up at that party. However, she hadn't come for the food and drink, but only to meet Jesus.

In the presence of Jesus the rottenness of her life suddenly hit her. Down came her tears in a flood, right on top of his tired and dusty feet. She looked around for a towel, but no one gave her one. So she dried his feet with her hair, and covered them with kisses. Then she produced a jar of ointment and anointed his feet with the ointment.

Simon was red with embarrassment. He despised the woman, and by his attitude of disdain let her know this. Thus in a thoughtless and selfish way he drove a dagger into an already deeply-wounded heart. He was shocked to see that instead of chasing her away, Jesus accepted her service. He was thinking, 'If this man was a holy man, he would know the kind of woman she is, and wouldn't allow her to touch him.'

But Jesus said to him, 'Simon, let me tell you something. When I entered your house, you gave me no water to wash my feet. But this woman washed my feet with her tears and dried them with her hair. You gave me no kiss of peace either. But she got down on her knees and kissed my feet. Neither did you think it worth your while to put some perfume on my head. But she has anointed my feet with ointment.' Then turning to the woman, he said, 'Your sins are forgiven. Go in peace.' (Luke 7:36-50).

❦

Simon looked at the woman and saw a sinner who would always be a sinner. Jesus looked at her and saw a sinner who was capable of becoming a saint. Simon looked at her and saw the 'mud'. Jesus looked at her and saw the wounds. His kindness was medicine for those wounds.

He didn't have to confront her with her sins. She was already painfully aware of them. Nor did he judge or condemn her. He saw that she had already been judged and punished by life. What she needed was healing, not condemnation.

He saw that there was another and better side to her. By graciously accepting her service, he helped her to believe in that side and to let it unfold. Had he refused her service and treated her with disdain, he would have sent her back to the darkness from which she had come.

In the heart of every person there is a core of goodness. It is on this that the future has to be built. This woman possessed that core too. Jesus was able to put her in touch with that in herself. The greatest good we can do for other people is not to give them of our own wealth but to show them their own.

The sheer goodness of Jesus made her feel that she too was good, and made her want to be like him. She had never experienced anything like this before. Jesus was the best person she had ever met. She was so happy that she was almost frightened of her happiness. As she went away, she was, as the Africans say, walking again with the moon and the stars.

## Invitation to Love

A MAN had a dream that he died and came before God to be judged. Holding out his hands he said, 'Lord, I've done nothing wrong. See, my hands are clean.' And God said, 'Yes, but they are empty.' Sometimes you hear people say, 'I haven't done anyone any harm.' They seem to regard this as the highest criterion of virtue. But it is a negative criterion. Jesus had a different criterion. It consisted not merely in avoiding evil but in doing good.

❦

Once a young man came to Jesus and asked, 'Good master, what must I do in order to gain eternal life?'

'Keep the commandments,' Jesus replied. 'Do not kill; Do not commit adultery; Do not steal; Do not bear false witness against anyone; Honour your father and your mother.'

'I've kept all of these since I was a child,' the man replied.

Jesus looked at him with love and admiration, and said, 'You still lack one thing.'

'What's that?' the young man asked earnestly.

'If you want to be perfect, sell everything you own, give the money to the poor, and you will lay up treasure for yourself in heaven. Then come back and follow me.'

On hearing this, the young man grew downcast, and went away sad, for he was very rich. (Mark 10:17-22).

❧

Why did the young man come to Jesus in the first place? Many a young person in his position would have been more than happy with his lot. He came because he admired Jesus; he called him 'Good master'. And he came because he was still searching. His heart had not yet been hardened by riches.

He asked, 'What must I *do* to gain eternal life?' As a young person, he longed for action. This would have endeared him to Jesus. And he had firm ground under his feet. He could say in all truth, 'I have kept all the commandments.'

Here undoubtedly was a good-living, respectable young man – the kind of son any parent could be proud of. A model? Yes – up to a point. He hadn't killed anyone; hadn't stolen from anyone; hadn't committed adultery; hadn't borne false witness against anyone; and hadn't dishonoured his father or mother. In short, he hadn't done anyone any harm.

We certainly are dealing with a good young man, one who has no blot on his copybook. But an outstanding young man? A young man who has been through the mill and proved himself? No. He simply has not been tested. But he is about to be tested.

For Jesus keeping the commandments was the bare minimum. He saw that the young man was capable of more. He offered him a new vision of goodness – a positive one. He said to him, 'If you want to be perfect, sell what you have. Give it to the poor. Then come back and follow me, and you will have treasure in heaven.'

But the young man was not up to it, and went away sad. Why sad? Sadness falls on those who say 'no' to love, and choose to live for themselves.

The challenge Jesus issued to him caused a vision of true greatness to flare up in his generous young heart. However, the price was too high. So he returned to his old comforts and securities. But he didn't return the same man. He returned stripped of illusions. He had traded his dreams for money and security.

Jesus saw that the rich young man had great potential. He wanted to free him from his addiction to possessions, and invited him to enter the world of sharing. But riches got in the way, with the result that his potential would lie dormant forever.

Even though Jesus was sad to see him go, nevertheless, he let him go. He respected his freedom. A love that denies freedom denies something sacred to God. We are the only creatures who can say 'no' to God. But we are also the only creatures who can return God's love. However, we can't love without freedom.

Virtue has great power but only when it is chosen. Hence, there is no point in forcing people to make sacrifices. What people give of their own accord is far more precious than what they give at the command or suggestion of others. If you take things away from people, they are impoverished. But if you can get them to give them up freely, they are enriched. People are essentially good. But this goodness has to be awakened and called forth if they are to enter the kingdom of love.

❦

There is a message in the story of the rich young man for everyone, but perhaps especially for the young. Why for the young in particular? Because generally the young are idealistic. They want to change the world. The first thing they have to realise is that they can't change the world. However, they can do something. But they had better do it quickly, before the world changes them.

## The Changing of a Heart

WHEN we hear about someone being converted we tend to assume that we are dealing with an intellectual conversion. In other words, we see conversion as affecting the head only. And while there are many edifying stories about people who underwent that kind of conversion, they apply to a relatively small number of people. But there is another kind of conversion which is relevant, and indeed essential, for all of us, namely, conversion of heart.

❦

Once Jesus was passing through Jericho. The whole town turned out to welcome him. Everyone was surprised when a man by the name of Zacchaeus showed up. Zacchaeus was a senior tax collector and a wealthy man. His lifestyle was in complete contrast to everything Jesus stood for. But the fact that he showed up at all shows that he must have secretly admired Jesus. This means that there was still a spark of goodness in his heart. Jesus would not extinguish that spark. Rather, he would seek to fan it into a flame.

Now Zaccheus just wanted to see what Jesus looked like. But since he was a small man, he had no hope of seeing Jesus if he stayed among the crowd. So he ran on ahead and climbed a sycamore tree in the hope of catching a glimpse of him as he passed by.

When Jesus reached the tree he looked up and saw Zacchaeus. No doubt the people expected and hoped that he would read the riot act to him. They hated Zacchaeus, and wanted to see him condemned and punished.

But Jesus did not read the riot act to Zacchaeus. He saw that what Zacchaeus needed was not condemnation but salvation. Addressing him in a kindly manner he said, 'Zacchaeus, come down. I want to stay in your house today.' And Zacchaeus hurried down and welcomed him with joy. The people took a very dim view of this. They complained that Jesus had gone to stay at the house of a sinner.

Later that day, as Jesus was leaving, Zacchaeus declared, 'Look, sir, I am going to give half my property to the poor, and if I have cheated anybody I will pay him back four times the amount.' And Jesus said, in the hearing of the people, 'Today salvation has come to this house. This man too is a son of Abraham. The Son of Man has come to seek out and save what was lost.' (Luke 19:1-10).

❦

What happened to Zacchaeus? He was converted. But his was not an intellectual conversion. It was a conversion to goodness. In other words, he had a change of heart. This is the most important conversion of all. It is harder to achieve than an intellectual conversion, and is more far reaching in its consequences. A change of heart is the most powerful agent of growth and transformation.

How does one bring about such a conversion? It can't be produced by fear. A harsh approach won't work; it only causes the heart to close and harden. It can be achieved only by love. Some doors open only from the inside. The door of the heart is one such door.

It takes goodness to evoke goodness. To get the best out of a person one has to find a way of touching that person's heart. All people have a core of decency, and are capable of changing if their hearts are touched. 'Speak to people's hearts, and they suddenly become virtuous' (Ralph Waldo Emerson).

We never improve people by rejecting them. A cold climate does not encourage growth. But extraordinary things happen when a climate of love is present. Therapists know that it is very difficult for change to happen except in a climate of acceptance. It is one of the great paradoxes that people don't change unless they feel accepted as they are.

Had Jesus snubbed Zacchaeus, the miracle would never have happened. But by coming to his house, in the face of the angry disapproval of the townspeople, Jesus showed Zacchaeus that he cared about him.

Zacchaeus had come in order to see what Jesus looked like. Well, by the end of the day, he had got a lot more than he bargained for or hoped for. Instead of getting a mere passing glimpse of Jesus, he had a face-to-face, and a heart-to-heart encounter with him.

He not only discovered what Jesus looked like but also what his heart was like. And to know the heart of Jesus was to know the possibilities of his own heart too. Zacchaeus liked what he discovered about Jesus. And he also liked what he discovered about himself. He experienced a great warmth in his heart. Suddenly his heart burst into life like a desert landscape after a rainfall.

And he experienced a joy the likes of which he had never experienced before. How do we know? Because he immediately decided to share some of his ill-gotten money with the poor. The first sign of happiness in the human heart is the desire to share with others.

ꙮ

The story of Zacchaeus is a story of redemption. It shows us how a good man lost himself and found himself again. It demonstrates how the power of love can transform a person.

Each of us has an innate capacity to love. Unfortunately, this love often lies hidden and unexpressed. Why is this? Because all of us are handicapped in one way or another. We have hands and we don't give, eyes and we don't see, ears and we don't hear, tongues and we don't speak, feelings and we don't show them. The greatest handicap of all, however, is a crippled heart.

A paraplegic observed: 'Living as a cripple in a wheelchair allows you to see more clearly the crippled hearts of some people whose bodies are whole and whose minds are sound.' Hence, each of us stands in daily need of a conversion from a closed heart to an open heart, from a heart of stone to a heart of flesh.

# A Lesson in Compassion

SHORTLY before the Second World War a Jewish community in Eastern Europe got news of an impending pogrom. The first thing they did was to take all the children to a safe house. It was the middle of winter and it was bitterly cold. The first night in the shelter there was one boy who was so cold and frightened that he couldn't sleep. A kind adult, who was keeping an eye on the children, noticed that this boy was still awake. He took off his own coat and placed it over the boy. Many years later, the boy, now an old man, related the story. 'You know,' he said, 'it's been over sixty years since that man spread his coat over me, but it still keeps me warm.'

It is hard to underestimate the value of kindness. Kindness is welcome at all times and in all situations. But it is like manna from heaven when one is vulnerable and exposed. In his Gospel, St John tells of the kindness Jesus showed to one who was in just that kind of situation.

❦

Once the Scribes and Pharisees brought a woman to Jesus. Forcing her to stand in full view of everybody, they said, 'Master, this woman was caught in the very act of committing adultery. Now, Moses has ordered us in the Law to condemn a woman like this to death by stoning. What do you say should be done with her?'

They asked this to test him. If he said, 'Go ahead and stone her,' he would lose the reputation he had among the people as a kind man, and people would no longer follow him. And if he said, 'Do not stone her,' he would be telling the people to break the Law of Moses, and then they could bring a definite charge against him. That was the trap they had set for him. There appeared to be no escape. He had to say 'yes' or 'no'.

But Jesus surprised them by saying nothing. Instead, he bent down and started writing on the ground with his finger. Nobody knows what he wrote. Maybe he didn't write anything. Maybe he just made some doodles. But they persisted: 'Come on, answer our question.' Finally he looked up and said, 'Let the one among you who has never sinned throw the first stone at her.' Then he bent down and went on writing on the ground.

When they heard this they went away one by one, beginning with the eldest, until Jesus was left alone with the woman, who remained standing there. He looked up and said, 'Woman, has no one condemned you?' 'No one, sir,' she replied. And he said, 'Well then, neither will I condemn you. Go away, and sin no more.' (John 8:1-11).

❦

On the surface there appears to be only one sin involved here – the sin of adultery. But on looking deeper we see that there are other sins present. There is the horrible sin involved in the way the Scribes and Pharisees treated the woman. They hadn't the slightest regard for her feelings, not the tiniest shred of concern for her as a person. They were merely using her as a bait with which to entrap Jesus. To use another person in this way is a despicable thing.

Then there is the sin involved in their attitude towards Jesus. Here were men who had only one thing in mind – to get rid of Jesus.

Yet, in spite of the way they shamed and humiliated the woman, and the murderous attitudes they harboured towards himself, there was something marvellously gentle and subtle in the way Jesus dealt with them. He did not condemn them. He didn't even judge them. Instead, he invited them to judge themselves. Reluctantly they were forced to confront their own sinfulness. And one by one they slunk away.

Jesus, the only sinless one among them, refused to condemn the woman. Why did he not condemn her? He distinguished between the sin and the sinner. He condemned the sin but pardoned the sinner. Besides, he knew that she had already been condemned. What she needed now was mercy. But someone might ask: did she deserve mercy? It would not be mercy if she deserved it. Of its nature, mercy is pure gift.

Nor did Jesus shame her. He said to her, 'Go and sin no more.' This shows he didn't deny her sin or take it lightly. By his gentle attitude he helped her to take responsibility for it. He corrected her, but showed that there is an art in doing so. This consists in being totally honest and totally kind at the same time. He treated her in such a way that it made her want to reform her life. 'Treat people as they are and they will become worse; treat them as they ought to be, or as they aspire to be, and they will become better' (Goethe).

But for Jesus the incident would, in all probability, have ended up with the woman lying as a bleeding mass on the ground. Who would have benefited from that? No one. All would have gone away diminished. Thankfully it ended very differently. No one died and all were taught a salutary lesson. Jesus illuminated a dark scene with the radiance of his kindness.

❧

The lovely thing about a kindness done to us is that it continues to benefit us long afterwards, through the memory we have of it. It becomes a spring to which we can return, and which never fails to refresh us. And the lovely thing about a kindness we do to another is that it benefits us as much as the one for whom we do it. When we treat another person kindly a sweetness falls like dew into our heart.

# The Fall and Rise of Peter

WE love to hear other people's stories. Why is this? Undoubtedly one reason is curiosity. But I believe there is a deeper reason. Whether we realise it or not, we hope to learn something about ourselves from them. Let us listen, then, to the story of the fall and the rise of Peter, and see what we can learn about ourselves from it.

❧

After the last supper, Jesus and his apostles left for the Mount of Olives. On the way there he said to them, 'Tonight all of you will lose faith in me.' On hearing this Peter said, 'Even if all the others lose faith in you, I will never lose faith in you.'

Those were brave words. And it's clear that Peter meant them.

But for all that, they still were only words. It's easy to be generous with one's words – words cost nothing. However, sooner or later all words are put to the test. Peter's fine words would soon be put to the test, and would come back to haunt him.

Peter thought he was brave and strong – stronger than any of the others. Jesus, who knew him through and through, tried to forewarn him, saying, 'Tonight, before the cock crows, you will have disowned me three times.' But Peter repeated still more earnestly, 'Even if I have to die with you, I will never disown you.' (Mark 14: 27-31).

How little he knew himself. Before the night was over he would find out some very painful truths about himself.

❦

Later that night in the garden of Gethsemane, Jesus was sorrowful, lonely, and fearful. He was in desperate need of some human companionship. So he took Peter, James and John with him, and said to them, 'My soul is ready to die with sorrow. Wait here and watch with me.' Going on a little further he fell on his face and prayed, 'Father, if it be possible, let this chalice pass from me. But not my will but thine be done.' When he came back to the apostles he found them sleeping.

Watching alongside someone who is suffering is no easy thing, especially when there is nothing you can do, and often nothing you can say either. Yet, in itself, what Jesus was asking of Peter was not a big thing – just to be present with him. It didn't call for heroism; only for a little ordinary courage. The bottom line was: stay awake. But Peter couldn't manage even that much. He fell asleep. How could anyone sleep on a night like that?

Here we have the first testing of Peter. In this moment of unbearable agony, Jesus turned to him, hoping to find support, but he was not with him. He was sleeping. He left him to drink the cup of sorrow alone. It was a poor show on Peter's part, coming so soon after his fine words.

Jesus was disappointed in him, and let him know it. Waking him up he said to him, 'Can you not watch even one hour with me?' However, he didn't make a big deal of it. In fact, he seemed to excuse it by adding, 'The spirit is willing, but the flesh is weak.' But his gentle reproof didn't register with Peter, because he went right back to sleep. (Mark 14:32-42).

❦

A short while later a number of men armed with swords and clubs, sent by the chief priests and elders of the people, arrived on the scene. They seized Jesus and took him to the house of the high priest. Peter followed along, at a safe distance, right into the courtyard of the high priest's house.

Since the night was cold they had lit a fire in the middle of the courtyard. Peter joined a group of people who were warming themselves at the fire, where he could see without, he hoped, being seen. The second and severest testing of Peter was about to take place.

A servant girl saw him and said, 'This man was with him too.'

But Peter denied it, saying, 'I do not know him.' Shortly afterwards someone else saw him and said, 'Aren't you one of his? Weren't you with him in the garden?' But Peter replied, 'I am not.'

Later another man said, 'This fellow was certainly with him. Why, you can tell by his accent that he is a Galilean.' At this Peter began to call down curses on himself and said, 'I swear, I do not know this man.'

No sooner had he said this than the cock crew. At that very moment Jesus was being led from the house of the high priest. He turned and looked at Peter. In a flash the words Jesus had spoken came back to Peter: 'Before the cock crows you will have denied me three times.' No doubt his own brave words came back too. How hollow they sounded now.

Jesus just looked at Peter. No words were said. But a look can be mightily effective. It can raise a person up or reduce a person to the size of a grain of sand. What was in the look of Jesus? It can't have been a look of condemnation. It must have been a look of compassion, because it made Peter realise exactly what he had done – he had denied his friend. He felt sick about it. And he went outside and wept bitterly. It was the lowest moment in his life. (Luke 22:54-62).

❦

After rising from the dead Jesus appeared to the apostles by the sea of Galilee. Now, after what happened in the garden and in the courtyard of the high priest's house, we would have expected Jesus to write off Peter as being weak, cowardly, and unreliable.

Yet after breakfast Jesus turned to him and said, 'Peter, do you love me more than the others love me?' What a strange question to ask: 'Do you love me?' Hadn't he proved beyond any shadow of doubt that he didn't love him? Yet this is the question Jesus asked Peter.

Chastened by failure, Peter would now speak only for himself. 'Lord, you know that I love you,' he answered. He sincerely meant those words, and what's more, they were true. He really did love Jesus. Judas' betrayal was a planned thing, and was carried out in a cold, calculating manner. Peter's denial was not a planned thing, and was the result of weakness rather than malice. But he didn't fall simply because he is weak. He fell because he thought he was strong.

Jesus accepted Peter's declaration of love and said to him, 'Feed my lambs.' However, he turned to Peter again and said, 'Simon, son of John, do you love me?' And Peter answered, 'Yes, Lord, you know I love you.' And Jesus said, 'Feed my sheep.'

A third time Jesus turned to him and said, 'Simon, son of John, do you love me?' Peter was upset that Jesus had asked him a third time, 'Do you love me?', and said, 'Lord, you know all things; well then, you must know that I love you.' And Jesus said to him, 'Feed my lambs and my sheep.' (John 21:1-17).

❦

Jesus did not write Peter off. He knew that there was another and better side to him. In spite of his weakness, his heart was sound. That one passing unfaithfulness would dissolve in his basic goodness, just as one drop of vinegar does not sour the whole container. Therefore, he restored a wiser and humbler Peter to where he was before, and made him the chief shepherd of his flock.

In giving authority to the man who denied him, Jesus showed that he was establishing his Church not on human strength, but on his own love and faithfulness.

This time Peter did not fail Jesus. It was he who led the apostles in witnessing to the resurrection. Few things help an individual more than to place responsibility on him, and to let him know that you trust him.

Jesus kept no record of Peter's sins. But he did ask him to do something for him. He asked him to feed the sheep and lambs of his flock, that is, to love and serve his brothers and sisters in the community. That is the best way to make atonement for sin. Peter himself later wrote, 'Love covers a multitude of sins' (I Pet. 4:8).

I'm sure that Peter never forgot the fact that he denied Jesus. Yet I doubt if it haunted him the way some people are haunted by their sins. Why was this? Because he learned from his fall. When we learn from a fall, the recalling of it is more likely to evoke gratitude than self-recrimination.

What did Peter learn from his fall? Firstly, he learned a very painful truth about himself. He learned that he wasn't as strong, or as brave, or as generous as he thought he was.

Secondly, he learned a wonderful truth about Jesus. He learned that in spite of his denials, Jesus still loved him. It was love that enabled him to turn an hour of pain and shame into an hour of grace and salvation.

To be loved in one's goodness is no big deal; but to be loved in one's sinfulness is a wonderful experience. It is in our sins that we experience the love and mercy of God. 'First there is the fall, and then there is the recovery from the fall. Both are the mercy of God' (Julian of Norwich).

❦

So what can we learn from the story of Peter's fall and rise?

Firstly, we learn how tenuous is the foothold we have on virtue, and how easy it is to fall. All of us are put to the test, but it never comes in the form and at the point we expect. We may have high principles, yet when the crunch comes we find we are unable to live up to them. We never know how we will react in a given situation until we are in that situation. What we are and what we think we are can be two very different things.

Secondly, we learn that it is possible to get up again after a fall and to put it behind us. The past is not denied, but remembered, forgiven, and redeemed. Our failures and betrayals can be transformed into gratitude, enabling us to become messengers of hope to others.

We are attracted to Peter because the frailties we see in him we recognise in ourselves. Peter is a great consolation to us. Courage fails us all. In the end, all of us are mere mortals who are inconstant in our beliefs. We need someone who understands our weaknesses, who realises that it may take time for us to overcome them, and who doesn't write us off because we don't produce the goods at once. And we must not judge ourselves or others by momentary lapses, but by commitment over a long time to our beliefs.

## A Traitor in Their Midst

HUMAN evil is a dark mystery. Sometimes evil is done openly, brazenly, and on a colossal scale. It is terrifying when done like this. We think of Hitler and his henchmen who were responsible for the deaths of some six million Jews. But at other times evil is done quietly, subtly, and on a much smaller scale. It is no less shocking when done like this. The shock may be caused, not so much by the evil that is done, but by the source from which it comes.

❧

The night before he died Jesus sat at table with his apostles. At a certain point he looked at them and said sadly, 'One of you is about to betray me'

He was deeply upset. He had personally chosen and trained these men. They had heard all his teaching and witnessed all his miracles. Yet now one of them was about to betray him. One of them had accepted thirty pieces of silver from the chief priests and elders to hand him over. The treachery of a friend is much more hurtful than the treachery of an enemy. 'Is it not a deadly sorrow when a comrade or a friend turns enemy?' (Sirach 37:2).

Now it was the turn of the apostles to get upset. It grieved them to think that one of their number could do such a thing. In betraying Jesus, the betrayer was betraying them too. One after another they asked, 'Is it I, Master?'

Taking a piece of bread, Jesus said, 'It is the man to whom I will give this piece of bread. Alas for the man by whom the Son of Man is betrayed. It would be better for him if he had never been born.' These are terrible words, but no doubt they were meant as a warning and not as a threat.

The apostles were now more upset than ever. But they were no nearer to knowing who the traitor was. John was sitting next to Jesus. Peter signalled to him to ask once more. So John said to Jesus, 'Master, tell us who it is.'

Jesus didn't answer. Instead, he dipped a piece of bread in the dish, and handed it to Judas. (The act of offering a piece of bread dipped in the dish was a gesture of courtesy for an honoured guest). Then he said to him, 'Be quick about what you're going to do.' None of the others understood the meaning of these words. They thought Jesus was sending Judas on an errand. Judas got up from the table and left the room. By now night had fallen. And night had fallen in the heart of Judas too. Darkness descends on the one who knowingly does what is wrong.

Jesus knew what Judas was up to. Yet he refused to expose him in front of the others. Everything remained between him and Judas. Thus he left the door open for him to return to the fold. A number of times during that last night he tried to reach him. He tried again in the garden.

There a mob armed with swords and clubs emerged from the darkness to arrest him. What a shock the apostles must have got when they saw who was at the head of that mod. It was none other than Judas, their fellow disciple, their friend, their brother. It was he who identified Jesus in the dark, doing so with a kiss.

Jesus' reaction was to say to him, 'Judas, my friend, do you betray the Son of Man with a kiss?' The words made no impression on Judas. By now he was past the point of rescue. (John 13:21-31; Matthew 26:23-24.50; Luke 22:47).

❧

Judas was chosen to be a witness to the light, yet he ended up in darkness. Can we shed any light on his journey into darkness?

We can presume that his heart was bright to begin with, bright with generosity and idealism. At what stage, then, did the darkness begin to invade this precious space? He must have taken a wrong turning somewhere along the way. We don't know what the first step was. But no doubt it was of no seeming consequence – just one of those small acts of cowardice with which a lot of terrible things begin.

He didn't suddenly turn against Jesus. There must have been a gradual dimming of the light. One doesn't suddenly become a scoundrel, unless one has already been one in the making. His journey into the night began some time back. But it was only on the last night that the full extent of the darkness became apparent. It would appear that he was not a man who looked back to see where his way of life was leading him. Is there a boundary that no one must cross lest he lose his soul?

Judas knew what he was doing. He knew that Jesus was innocent. His act was not the result of a sudden impulse or fit of passion. It was a planned thing, and was carried out in a cold, calculating manner. Moreover, he saw how it affected Jesus. Nevertheless, he went ahead with it.

Judas became something worse than an enemy. He became a traitor. But he didn't set out to become a traitor. Nor did God predestine him for that role. He became a traitor through the choices he made. He set out with a dream. But something went wrong. What exactly that was we'll never know. The only clue the Gospel gives us is that before he became a traitor he became a thief (John 12:6).

Judas was not a demon but a bad man. A bad man is made from human material that might have become something very different. There must have been good in him, otherwise Jesus would not have chosen him in the first place. Besides, he had given up everything to follow Jesus. Now he is doomed to be remembered forever by one dark deed.

And yet Judas was not so lost as not to be able to tell the difference between light and darkness. Next day when he learned that Jesus had been condemned to death, he was filled with remorse, and took the thirty silver pieces back to the chief priests and elders, saying, 'I have sinned in betraying an innocent man' (Matthew 27:3). But he got no sympathy from them. Then he went off and hanged himself.

No one has ever explained what motivated Judas to do what he did. It remains an incomprehensible and unfathomable riddle. But one thing is clear: Jesus never rejected him. On the contrary, he loved him to the end.

But by this is sentence passed on him, that even though he was exposed to the light, he opted for the darkness. Nevertheless, probably the worst thing he did was to despair. Peter denied Jesus but returned to him in tears. Judas betrayed Jesus, then ran away from him in despair and hanged himself.

❦

Judas fascinates us because he must have once been a good man.

After the war some of the Nazis leaders were tracked down and arrested. What did they find? Devils incarnate? Madmen? No, they found human beings who were perfectly sane, and who belonged to the same human family as ourselves. This is what frightens us.

We look at them and see something of ourselves, of our cowardice, our failures, our betrayals, and our need of grace. All of us have a dark side. There are many degrees of darkness and many shades of night, but darkness of heart is the blackest night of all. And it is darker when the light goes out than if it had never shone.

# It Is Never Too Late

E VERYBODY loves a beautiful sunset. But here is a thing that may surprise some. The most beautiful sunsets occur, not when the sky is cloudless, but when there are some clouds in the sky. The clouds reflect the light of the dying sun and scatter it across the sky, sometimes in a dazzling variety of colours.

I recall an August day in America. During the morning there was thunder and lightning and bouts of heavy rain. During the afternoon it got hot and sticky. The evening was murky and miserable. Yet just when the curtain was about to come down on the day something beautiful occurred. There came a stunning sunset. What had been an ugly day ended in beauty.

It reminds me of something that happened on Calvary.

❦

Jesus was crucified between two thieves. The people stood there watching them as they hung on the crosses. The leaders taunted him, saying, 'He saved others, let him now save himself if he is the Christ of God.' The soldiers mocked him, saying, 'If you are the king of the Jews, save yourself.'

Even one of the thieves joined in the mockery. He said, 'If you are the Messiah, save yourself and us too.' But the other thief rebuked him, saying, 'Have you no fear of God at all? We got the same sentence as he did, but in our case we deserved it: we are paying for what we did. But this man has done nothing wrong.'

Then he turned to Jesus and said, 'Jesus, remember me when you come into your kingdom.'

And Jesus said, 'I promise you, today you will be with me in Paradise.' (Luke 23:33-43).

❦

The first of the thieves is a profoundly disturbing character. Even with death staring him in the face, he didn't show a trace of remorse, the least gnawing of conscience. There was no pity or humanity left in this scornful and wretched man. He showed how low he had sunk by joining in the mockery of Jesus. It seems that even Jesus was powerless to save him. No one can save the person who doesn't want to be saved.

Powerlessness is very painful for a caring person. Doctors are familiar with this pain. There are times when even the greatest doctors are powerless to save a life. It is never easy for a doctor to admit to being powerless. Doctors are trained to heal, and almost instinctively see the death of a patient as a defeat. But in time they learn to accept their limitations, and continue to do what they can.

The second thief is a very interesting character. He showed that there was still some decency left in him when he rebuked his companion and spoke up for Jesus. As he hung on the cross, he did a quick review of his life. And what did he see? He saw a heap of rubble. He had wasted his life. And it was now too late to do anything about it.

Yet here is an amazing thing. He made no excuses. Nor did he blame others for the predicament in which he found himself. Today there is a disturbing tendency to take responsibility away from the individual. It is common to blame someone else. The thief might have blamed his upbringing, his environment, his companions. But he didn't. He took full responsibility for the person he had become.

What he did was a tremendous thing. It involved something that is never easy – radical honesty with oneself. But to do it in the atmosphere that prevailed on Calvary makes it still greater, given the taunting of the religious leaders, and the mocking of the soldiers and his comrade.

Now the curtain was going down on his murky life. Everything was dark and hopeless. The past offered no solace; the future no promise. So who could he turn to? No one but Jesus, the friend of sinners. The goodness of Jesus awakened his own lost goodness. The forgotten man within him came to life again, and he became, at least for a fleeting moment, the man he ought to have been. Turning to Jesus, he said, 'Remember me when you come into your kingdom.' It was a beautiful act of faith in Jesus, and at the same time a recognition of his own absolute poverty.

'Remember me!' That was all he said. But that said it all. It was a cry from the heart. And Jesus did not disappoint him. Seeing the sad tatters of his life, Jesus was moved with compassion for him and said, 'This day you will be with me in paradise.' These are wonderful words because in them is hope of salvation for every person. On hearing them the sky of the thief's life suddenly became resplendent with hope.

How come Jesus was able to reach the second thief but not the first? The answer lies in the different attitudes they adopted. There is a proverb which states: 'The nature of rain is the same, yet it produces thorns in the marsh and flowers in the garden.'

The difference between the two thieves came down to the heart. The heart of the first thief was hard, embittered, and inaccessible. It was a dry heart, a heart that could form no tears. The heart of the second thief was still open, still capable of recognising and responding to goodness. Thanks to his encounter with Jesus, he found peace and hope at the end. He still died, but he died a different person.

❦

There is a saying that says: as a person lives so shall he die. No doubt there is truth in this. But it is far too simplistic. Besides, it leaves no room for grace. As long as we breathe there is no final verdict on our lives.

The story of the repentant thief gives hope to everyone, but especially to those who come to the end of life and have nothing that they can feel good about. Salvation is always a gift from God. God gives it most freely to those who, like the repentant thief, know they are poor, and who ask for it with empty hands and expectant hearts.

## The Victory of Love over Hate

DENIS and Anne lived in New York City and had been happily married for forty years. Unfortunately in his later years Denis' health was very poor. He was constantly in and out of hospital with a number of different complaints. All this time Anne remained totally devoted to him, while keeping down a job at the same time. Eventually he suffered a stroke and had to go to a nursing home.

Liam, a friend of both of them, used to visit Denis on Sundays. Anne also visited him, but usually Liam would get there first. I'll let him tell the rest of the story.

'I would be sitting there, chatting with him, and we would hear Anne's footsteps coming down the hallway. I could see the relaxation in his face on hearing those footsteps. Sadly, a few months later Anne was struck by a car and killed. Everybody knew that this was the end of Denis – and it was. A week after the funeral he had a major setback and was taken to hospital.

When I visited him he looked neglected, helpless, and forlorn. As I was sitting by his bedside we heard footsteps coming down the hallway. His eyes sparkled for a moment, thinking that they were Anne's. But of course he soon realised that they were not.

With that a look came over his face, the likes of which I've never seen in my life. The only way I can describe it is to say that it was a look of utter broken-heartedness. Then he sank back into the bed. Even if you told him at that moment that he had won the lottery, it wouldn't have made the slightest difference to him. Twenty-four hours later he was dead.'

☙

The hour of parting is frequently a painful hour. But it can also be a blessed hour because it is an hour of heightened sensibility. It causes us to focus on essentials. In normal times we are reluctant to express our deepest feelings lest we be considered soft, but at the hour of parting they come gushing out in spite of us. 'Love knows not its own depth until the hour of separation' (Kahlil Gibran).

❧

The night before he died Jesus gathered the apostles around him, and ate a last supper with them. Reading about this supper in the Gospels, we get glimpses of the anguish he felt in his heart that night. We glimpse that anguish in the disappointment he felt at the fickleness of the apostles: 'Tonight all of you will abandon me' (Mark 14.27). And we glimpse it especially in the distress he felt at the thought that one of them would betray him: 'One of you is about to betray me' (John 13.21).

Yet he refused to shut them out of his heart. On the contrary, he opened his heart to them, saying, 'I will not call you servants any more ... I call you friends' (John 15.15). Then he said: 'I am the vine, you are the branches.' Here we have a beautiful image of closeness and interdependence.

Was it not a strange time to talk about unity when everything seemed to be falling apart? He went on to say, 'Love one another, as I have loved you' (John 13.34). And was it not a strange time to talk about love when love was being betrayed?

It goes without saying that it was a difficult night for the apostles too, a night filled with confusion and fear, a night it which their weaknesses were cruelly exposed. When Jesus began to talk about 'going away' they were overcome with sorrow. 'Going away' could mean only one thing – that he was going to die.

Seeing their sorrow, Jesus tried to comfort them, saying, 'Do not let your hearts be troubled. Trust in God still, and trust in me' (John 14:1). And he sowed hope amidst their tears when he said, 'There are many rooms in my Father's house; I am going to prepare a place for you. You are sad now; but I will see you again, and your hearts will rejoice, and your joy no one will take from you' (John 14:1;16:22).

The scene then shifts from the supper room to the garden of Gethsemane. Here we see Jesus at his most human. Some people insist that their hero must never show any sign of weakness. But heroes who never show weakness are simply not believable. A hero is no less a hero because he shows that he isn't made of stone.

Hitherto Jesus had gone resolutely to his fate. But now that the dreadful moment had arrived, he was overcome with anguish. He said, 'My soul is ready to die with sorrow.' His sweat fell to the ground like drops of blood. Three times he prayed: 'Father, if it be possible, let this cup pass from me. But not my will but thine be done.'

Eventually he found the strength to face what had to be faced. By that time Judas had arrived. With him was a band of men armed with swords and clubs. Jesus came forward to meet them and said, 'Who are you looking for?'

'Jesus of Nazareth,' they answered.

'I am Jesus of Nazareth,' he said. 'If it's me you're looking for, then let the others go free.'

Here we see how he cared about his friends to the end. Then he surrendered himself to the arresters, and they led him away. With that all the disciples deserted him and ran away. (Mark 14:32-42).

❦

During the years of his public ministry Jesus had always been in control. He had come and gone as he wished. But now that he was in the hands of his enemies everything was out of his control. And that is when his passion began. The very essence of suffering lies in the fact that the initiative is taken out of our hands.

Jesus was led in turn before Caiphas, Herod, and Pilate. He was interrogated, insulted, spat upon, flogged, crowned with thorns, condemned as a criminal, and given a cross to carry to the place of execution. A large crowd followed him on the way to Calvary. He must have been very weak because they enlisted a passer-by, Simon of Cyrene, to help him carry the cross.

Among the crowd was a group of women who were crying for him. But he turned to them and said, 'Don't cry for me. Cry for yourselves and for your children.' He wasn't rejecting their sympathy. He knew that Jerusalem would soon be destroyed, and was forewarning the women. In effect he was saying to them, 'My suffering is nothing compared to what yours will be. Prepare yourselves.'

It speaks volumes about the kind of person he was that from the depths of his own pain he could feel for the plight of those women. One's pain can so easily turn into rage, causing one to lash out blindly at whoever happens to be within range.

In describing the death of Jesus St Luke says, 'It was about noon and, with the sun eclipsed, a darkness came over the whole land until the ninth hour' (23:44). We don't know if he was talking about an actual darkness or just using darkness as a symbol to illustrate that Jesus, the Light of the world, was dying. But one thing is certain: Calvary was a dark place. It was made dark by mockery and hatred.

Yet, in spite of all this, Jesus' heart never closed or hardened. Even as he hung on the cross, it remained open, even to his enemies. He prayed for them with the words, 'Father, forgive them, for they know not what they do' (Luke 23:34). Helder Camara says that some people are like sugar-cane; even when crushed in the mill, completely squashed, reduced to pulp, all they yield is sweetness.

It is said that the only prize life offers in the end is a handful of people who love us. A small group of friends stayed with Jesus to the end. Among these was his mother, Mary, and the disciple, John. It must have been harrowing for them, especially for his mother. All they could do was stand there in silence. But their presence saved him from dying alone and abandoned.

Even so, as he died he experienced an intense feeling of abandonment by God, so much so that he cried out: 'My God, my God, why have you forsaken me?' (Mark 15:34). Nevertheless, he died with a prayer of trust on his lips: 'Father, into your hands I commend my spirit.' (Luke 23:46).

❦

Jesus was crucified on a Friday. That Friday might well have been called 'Bad Friday', because of the human wickedness that manifested itself on that day. But we don't call it 'Bad Friday'. We call it 'Good Friday'. Why? Because that dark day was made luminous by the goodness of Jesus. The death of Jesus may seem a defeat. It was not a defeat. It was a victory – the victory of love over hate.

As Christians, the cross is our most precious and sacred symbol. When we wish to invoke a blessing on someone we do so by making the sign of the cross over them. Many people wear the cross around their neck as a protection against evil. The cross stands atop our churches. And it will stand vigil over our graves.

The cross is a symbol of love and hope. It is a symbol of love because it reminds us of the words of Jesus: 'No one has greater love than the one who lays down his life for his friends' (John 15:13). It is a symbol of hope because we see it in the light of Easter.

## Footprints in the Snow

O N a winter's afternoon I went for a walk across fields covered with snow which glistened in the bright sunlight. My feet sank into the soft, clean snow. For a while I walked along in a kind of trance. But at a certain point I began to concentrate on the ground. It was then I noticed that the snow was full of tracks made by birds and animals. On looking closely at those tracks I was able to identify some of these birds and animals, and even to tell what they were up to.

Most of what I saw there was harmless – the tracks of little creatures struggling to stay alive in a hostile climate. For instance, I saw the scratchings of robins and sparrows in their quest for a worm. I saw the rootings of rabbits and hares looking for a blade of grass. I saw the beaten snow where sheep had passed. But then I saw a spatter of blood on the snow where a fox or a bird of prey had made a kill.

On a normal day you could cross and re-cross these fields, and you would see nothing of the doings of the birds and animals. Everything would be covered up. But today their cover was blown.

Everything was written there in the snow – innocence, fun, resourcefulness, pain, cunning, and red murder.

This can happen in the world of humans too. For instance, something happens in the neighbourhood or in the work-place, and people are forced to take a stand. Suddenly their cover is blown and their minds and hearts are revealed. Some come out well, but others are shown up in a poor light.

The trial of Jesus was such an event. Jesus was such a transparently good person that when he was put on trial, the snow of his innocence fell from heaven and covered the earth. All who were abroad on that day had their cover blown. All left clear and unmistakable tracks behind them.

When we look at those tracks we see some ugly things. We see the hatred and fanaticism of Caiphas and the religious leaders who plotted his death. We see the cold, calculating evil of Judas who betrayed him. We see the weakness of Peter who disowned him. We see the cruelty of Herod who mocked him. We see the cowardice of Pilate, who, though he knew he was innocent, signed his death warrant. We see the unthinking hostility of the mob who shouted: 'Crucify him! Crucify him!' We see the dutiful obedience of the soldiers who carried out the execution.

But we also see some beautiful things. We see the compassion of Veronica who wiped his face. We see the courage of Simon of Cyrene who helped him carry the cross. We see the sympathy of the women of Jerusalem who wept for him. We see the loyalty of a little group of friends who stayed with him to the end, among these were his mother and the disciple John.

It wasn't Jesus who was judged on that day. It was his disciples, and especially his accusers and executioners. But it wasn't he who judged them. They judged themselves – by the tracks they left behind.

❦

All of us leave tracks behind us. Every now and then we should put down our bags and examine those tracks. Are they the tracks of a coward, a hypocrite, someone who lives only for himself or herself? Or are they the tracks of a courageous person, a generous person, one who is not ashamed to be seen to be a disciple of Jesus? It is by the tracks we leave behind us that we will be remembered.

## Sorrow Turned into Joy

A DYING Buddhist monk asked a Catholic priest to instruct him in the truths of the faith. The priest complied with the monk's request. Afterwards the monk thanked him, but added, 'You filled my mind with beautiful thoughts, but you left my heart empty.' How well I know those presentations of the faith that leave you cold and empty because they provide, not vision and inspiration, but merely a compendium of facts.

ॐ

On Easter Sunday evening two of Jesus' disciples were returning home to Emmaus, a village about seven miles from Jerusalem. They were experiencing a terrible emptiness in their hearts. They had firmly believed that Jesus was the promised Messiah. But when he was crucified they where devastated. A humiliated, crucified Messiah was a contradiction in terms. They searched the Scriptures for answers but found none.

Their idea of the Messiah was that of an all-conquering hero, who would restore Israel to its former greatness. This was not Jesus' idea of the Messiah. On more than one occasion he had tried to tell his disciples in advance that the Messiah would suffer and be put to death, but they didn't want to know. (Matthew 16: 21; 17: 22-23; 20:18-19).

They made their way homewards, sad at heart and down in spirit. 'When the heart is sad the spirit is broken' (Proverbs 15:13). At a certain point a stranger joined them. 'What were you talking about as you walked along?' the stranger asked in a kindly manner. And they began to tell him their sad story.

They told him all about Jesus of Nazareth, and the great things he had said and done among the people. They told him how the chief priests arrested him, and handed him over to the Romans who crucified him three days previously. They told him that early that morning some women disciples had gone to his tomb and found it empty, and claimed they had seen angels who declared that he was alive. Some of their friends had gone to the tomb and found that what the women said was true, but of him they saw nothing.

Only when they had finished did he start to talk. 'You foolish men!' he said. 'So slow to believe all that the prophets had said! Did you not know that the Messiah had to suffer in order to enter into his glory?' Then he opened their minds to a new way of looking at the Scriptures. He showed them how all the prophets from Moses onwards had foretold that the Messiah would suffer, and *thus* enter into glory.

The two listened with rapt attention. So absorbed were they in what he was saying that they didn't feel the miles going by. Before they knew it, they had reached Emmaus. By this time night was falling, but he made as if to go on. They invited him to stay with them, and he agreed to do so.

Later, when they were having supper, he took the cake of bread, blessed it, broke it, and gave each of them a piece – just as Jesus had done at the Last Supper. Suddenly their eyes were opened and they recognised the stranger. He was none other than Jesus! But at that moment he disappeared from their sight. Then they said to one another, 'We should have known all along that it was he! Were not our hearts burning within us as he explained the Scriptures to us?'

In spite of the lateness of the hour, they set off back to Jerusalem to share the good news with the apostles. Their beloved Jesus was alive, and had entered into glory! And what was that glory? It was his triumph over evil and death. So the death of Jesus, far from being the end of the dream, was precisely the way it was realised. Jesus was the Messiah, not in spite of his suffering, but because of it. (Luke 24:13-35).

What did Jesus do for those two disciples? He certainly illuminated their minds. But he did something even better. He set their hearts on fire. How did he do this? He placed himself alongside them. He listened to them. He accompanied them on their sad journey, and taught them about the goodness of God.

God makes all things work for the good of those who place their hope in him. God brings good out of evil, life out of death, and glory out of pain and suffering. God makes our deepest dreams come true in the most surprising of ways.

What the priest should have done for the dying monk was to give him an experience of Christian love. It is clear that it was not his mind that needed addressing so much as his heart. Beautiful thoughts can nourish the mind, but only love can nourish the heart. What he wanted was someone to listen to him, and to journey with him. 'In all my years of dealing with the dying there was not a single dying human being who did not yearn for love, touch or communication. If there was another human being who cared, they would arrive at acceptance' (Elizabeth Kubler-Ross).

And, of course, the priest should have told him the story of Jesus. The path that led Jesus to glory was not an easy one. But if it was easy it would not be of much use to us. There is no such thing as conferred glory. Glory can only be attained through struggle and suffering. The labour and pain with which a victory is surrounded is the best part of the joy afterwards. Yet it wasn't so much his death that earned Jesus that glory but the life of sacrifice and service that preceded it and from which it flowed.

❧

Even though we may never have been to the Holy Land, all of us have some experience of the road to Emmaus. 'Once at least in his life each man walks with Christ to Emmaus' (Oscar Wilde). The road to Emmaus represents the road of disappointment, failure, sorrow, grief, broken dreams.

But we are not alone on this road. The risen Lord journeys with us, even though we may not recognise him. He is so close to us that our stories merge with his. His resurrection opens all our stories to the prospect, not just of a good ending, but of a glorious ending. His story makes it possible for us to enter the dark kingdom of death with hearts that are filled with hope.

## The Leave-taking

B EFORE taking leave of the apostles, Jesus spoke more than once about his impending departure. In doing so he used a strange phrase. He said, 'It is for your own good that I leave. Unless I go, the Spirit will not come. But if I go, I will send him to you' (John 16:7).

The apostles found the idea that his leaving could be for their good incomprehensible. They saw his leaving as an unmitigated disaster, and the mere thought of it filled them with sorrow. How are we to understand these words of Jesus? The following illustration may shed some light on what he meant.

❦

One evening in late November I was walking along a certain road. The sky was clear and the air crisp. The sun was going down behind me, filling the landscape with its golden light as it did so. Yet in spite of the gold the sun radiated, the world had an over-familiar, worn-out and rusty appearance. Autumn had plundered it of all the fruits of summer.

At a certain point I looked at the sky. There, high to my right, I spotted the moon. Though it was almost full, it was so pale and weak as to be practically invisible. Having located it, I continued to gaze at it for some moments. It didn't appear to be contributing anything whatsoever to the earth.

Meanwhile the sun went on with its leave-taking. As it left it seemed to be taking the whole world with it. However, as it withdrew I noticed a curious and beautiful thing. The lower the sun dipped in the sky, the brighter the moon became. By the time the sun had finally departed the scene, the moon had undergone a complete transformation. It was now, far and away, the brightest object in the evening sky.

Of course, even at its zenith, it could not compare with the sun. Yet its silvery light was not only adequate to see by, but cast an enchantment over everything. As I looked around me I noticed to my surprise and delight that the old world had not only been completely restored to me, but had been made new, bright and exciting.

It was only when the sun had withdrawn that I could see what the moon was contributing. I was aware, of course, that it only reflected the light of the sun, now hidden from me. It still needed the sun, but the sun also needed it to reflect its light on the earth.

And I thought: that's what love does. Loving at times means distancing oneself from those we love. This leaves them free to develop in their own way as well as to receive from others. They come to realise that they have a unique contribution to make, and are given an opportunity to make it.

Alas, often we do the exact opposite. We hug the limelight. We want to be present all the time. We do not know when or how to withdraw. Thus in a thoughtless and selfish way we dominate others, keeping them in the shadows, and stifling their development. There is, however, an art in withdrawing. We have to withdraw in such a way that they know we are not abandoning them.

As I walked on I gazed once more at the moon. It was now shining so brightly that you would think it had a secret source of light within itself. Under its gentle light all sorts of little creatures who could not endure the heat of the sun had ventured out into the open. The night was alive with rustlings.

# The Genius of the Heart

ALL of the foregoing encounters have revealed to us aspects of the heart of Jesus. To sum them up would be impossible. The very least we can say is that Jesus was a genius of the heart. But how are we to describe a genius of the heart? I don't think that anyone could improve on the words of the German philosopher, Friedrich Nietzsche. I'm not sure if he had Jesus in mind when he wrote them, but if they apply to anyone, they surely apply to him. Anyway, here is what he had to say about the genius of the heart, the arrangement and editing is mine:

The genius of the heart ...
whose voice knows how to descend into the underworld
of every soul ...
who makes everything loud and self-satisfied fall silent
and teaches it to listen ...
who smooths rough souls ...
who teaches the stupid and hasty hand to hesitate
and grasp more delicately;
who divines the hidden and forgotten treasure,
the drop of goodness and sweet spirituality
under thick and opaque ice,
and is a divining rod for every grain of gold
which has lain long in the prison of much mud;
the genius of the heart
from whose touch everyone goes away richer ...
not as if blessed and oppressed with the goods of others,
but richer in themselves,
newer to themselves than before,
broken open,
blown upon ... by a thawing wind,
more uncertain perhaps,
more delicate,

more fragile,
more broken,
but full of hopes that as yet have no names.

(Adapted from *A Nietzsche Reader*, Penguin Books)

PART THREE

# *Parables*
# *of the Heart*

# The Resistant Heart and the Receptive Heart

IN the course of our lives we hear an enormous number of words. The vast majority of these go in one ear and out the other, and so have no effect on our lives. But some have a profound effect on our lives. Why is this? Because they go straight to our hearts.

❦

Jesus compared a word to a seed. He told a story about a man who went out to sow seed in his field. Some seed fell on a path which ran through the field. There the soil was rock-hard with the result that the seed was unable to put down roots. It lay on the surface, and the birds came and ate it. Other seed fell on stony ground where the soil was very shallow. It sprang up quickly, but when the weather got hot, it withered away for lack of roots. Other seed fell among thorns, and the thorns grew up and choked it. And other seed fell on good ground where it grew up and produced a harvest. (Matthew 13:4-9).

❦

Clearly the parable applies to all words. But Jesus was specifically talking about the word of God. The ground in which this precious seed is sown is the human heart. God's word is essentially an appeal to our hearts. God longs for our hearts, and is continually calling us into communion with him and with one another. Unfortunately, the heart is not always receptive.

The seed that fell on the beaten path represents those whose hearts are hard. Sadly, God's call makes no impression on them. A hard heart is a closed heart, so it can't receive. A hard heart inevitably becomes a barren heart.

The seed that fell on stony ground represents those whose hearts are resistant. God's call is heard alright but doesn't make a deep impression. When difficulties occur, it fades away.

The seed that fell among thorns represents those whose hearts are so full of worldly concerns that the call of God gets drowned out. It is not that God is deliberately excluded, but that there is no room for him.

And the seed that fell on good ground represents those who receive God's call with open and generous hearts, and in responding to it, produce a harvest of goodness.

❦

God doesn't speak to us the way a dictator speaks to his subjects. God's voice is a very gentle one. This is because it is the voice of love. Yet God's word can do what the word of the most powerful dictator cannot do – it can change our hearts.

In a *cri de coeur* the psalmist says to God's people: 'O that today you would listen to his voice! Harden not your hearts' (Psalm 95:8). We would do well to heed that cry. To harden our hearts against anyone is bad, but to harden them against God would be a calamity.

Jesus came, not just to purify our hearts, but to soften and warm them, so that they might be able to receive the word of God. Softened by the rain of his grace, and warmed by the sun of his love, the seed of God's word can take root in our hearts, and turn them from a desert into a garden.

# The Divided Heart

S OME years ago I was in England to preach a retreat. The retreat house had once been a house of formation for young Salesians. I myself had been a student there. As I walked up the long driveway, I found it hard to believe that thirty years had gone by since those days.

Later that evening I went into the chapel. There my mind went back to my student days, and I found myself reflecting on how I had changed in the intervening years. On the positive side, I had discovered talents in myself which back then I had no idea I possessed. On the negative side, I had discovered weaknesses in myself which had caused me an amount of trouble. Then one of

Jesus' parables came back to me.

᪥

It was about a farmer who sowed wheat in his field. But one night while he was asleep an enemy came and sowed weeds over the wheat. A couple of weeks went by, and up came the shoots of wheat, fresh and green and lovely. The farmer was delighted. It looked as if he was going to get a bumper harvest from the field. But then the weeds appeared.

On seeing the weeds, the farmer's workers went to him and said, 'Do you want us to go and pull up the weeds?' But he said, 'No. In pulling up the weeds, you would pull up some of the wheat as well.' 'So what are we to do?' they asked. 'We'll just have to let them both grow until the harvest-time,' he replied. 'Then we'll gather up the weeds into bundles and burn them, and the wheat we'll store in the barn.' (Matthew 13:24-30).

᪥

Thirty years ago I had no idea of the 'weeds' that lay dormant within me and that would one day awaken. Therefore, it never occurred to me to apply this parable to myself. I saw it as applying to the Church and to the world. But that evening as I gazed into the field of my life I realised that Jesus' parable applied to me too. In fact, it had come true for me. The wheat and weeds had grown together.

Even though this is an obvious truth, it can take a long time to grasp it. It is a humbling truth, yet there is a kind of freedom in knowing and accepting it. Once we have accepted our own limitations as human beings, there is nothing left to hide. There is no more need to play games or to pretend. It is a great relief when you are able to give up self-deception and be completely honest with yourself. The tolerance of one's dividedness comes as a great liberation.

However, some people never seem to take it on board. They have a tendency to idealise some people and demonise others. For them the world is populated by two distinct categories of people – saints and sinners. They have little or no understanding of the divided nature of each human being, and the complexity of the human heart. As soon as they discover a flaw or a weakness in someone, they write the person off. They never allow individuals to forget their past. For them one act of disloyalty outweighs anything else a person might do in his/her life. What does this tell us about them? It tells us that they have very little self-knowledge. The fact is: human beings are complex creatures. They can't be divided into saints and sinners. Such a division is quite unreal.

One man who came to a profound understanding of the entwined complexities and contradictions of people is Alexander Solzhenitsyn. In his monumental work, *The Gulag Archipelago*, he says:

> I learnt one great lesson from my years in prison camps. I learnt how a person becomes evil and how he becomes good. Gradually I came to realise that the line which separates good from evil passes not between states, or between classes, or between political parties, but right through every human heart. Even in hearts that are overwhelmed by evil, one small bridgehead of good is retained. And in the best of all hearts, there remains an unprooted small corner of evil. (*The Gulag Archipelago*, vol. 2)

Another man who came to understand it was Fyodor Dostoevsky. The four years he spent in a Siberian prison gave him an opportunity to observe people at close quarters. He saw the meanness and the generosity, the cruelty and the compassion that can coexist in the same human heart. Later he wrote, in *Memoris of the House of the Dead*:

> It sometimes happened in prison that you knew a man for several years, thought of him as a refined and educated man, and had a high regard for him. But then one day you discover that behind the facade lay such barbarism and cynicism that you were revolted. The opposite might also happen: you thought of a man as a brute and not a man at all, and despised him. Then suddenly a chance moment would reveal in his soul such wealth, such feeling and heart, that you would find it hard to

believe what you had seen and hear.

No one understood this better than Jesus. Even in the small garden (the apostolic group) which he tended lovingly for three years, the weeds persisted. Yet he didn't write it off. He refused to weed out Judas. He never rejected him, but loved him to the end. And he refused to weed out Peter. He saw the weeds in Peter's life – contradictions, flaws, and imperfections. But he saw the wheat too – generosity and capacity for leadership. He knew that with encouragement the wheat would prevail. And it did.

❦

The reality is that everyone is a mixture of light and shadow, good and evil. Each human heart is a divided kingdom. The sooner we come to terms with this the better. If the heart was completely unified it would make life very simple. But it is not. There is a war going on inside us, between altruism and egoism, between good and evil. This is what Paul was talking about when he said very candidly: 'I do not understand my own behaviour; I fail to carry out the things I want to do, and I find myself doing the very things I hate' (Romans 7:15).

When Jesus says that we must let the weeds grow, he is not saying that we must let evil have its way. Evil has to be resisted. However, this has to be done in such a way that we don't do further evil in the process. Evil can be overcome only by good.

So what must we do? We must acknowledge the presence of the weeds in the garden of the heart. But we must acknowledge that there is wheat there too. We must encourage the wheat every way we can, in the hope that it will outgrow the weeds. In practice this means seeking the good in ourselves and in others, revealing that good and bringing it out.

But we have to face the fact that we are never the complete masters of ourselves. We are involved in a constant struggle. But struggle is actually good for us. Cheap victories do little for us. Good appears most vividly in resistance to its opposite. That is what heroism is about.

❦

The Kingdom of God in the world and in the heart of each of us is still at the growing stage. The time for reaping the harvest is not yet. Now is the time for conversion. People are capable of changing. God is a lot more tolerant than we are. A person may make a great mistake, but by the grace of God redeem himself.

The day of death is the day of the harvest. On that day the harvest of our lives will be poured out before God. Naturally, each of us hopes that the harvest will be an abundant one. But the only thing that is certain is that it will consist of a mixture of wheat and weeds. We pray that the Lord's wise hand will sift through it, keeping what is worth keeping, and with the breath of his kindness blowing the rest away.

## The Empty Heart

THE painter, Vincent Van Gogh, experienced intense loneliness and anguish during his relatively short life. This was due mainly to the difficulty he had in relating to other people and his failure to win recognition as an artist. In a haunting image he describes just how lonely and empty his life was. 'There may be a great fire in our soul, but no one ever comes to warm himself at it, and the passers-by see only a little bit of smoke coming through the chimney, and pass on their way.'

What we are hearing here is a cry for love. It was his heart that was empty. Emptiness of heart is a sorry and dangerous state. It makes a person very vulnerable. Just as an empty house is an invitation for unwelcome guests to come and squat, so an empty heart makes a person vulnerable before the forces of evil.

❦

Jesus told a disturbing little story about an evil spirit which went out of a man and wandered through arid country looking for a suitable place to rest. Unable to find such a place, it decided to return to its original abode. When it came back it found the place swept and tidied, but empty. So the spirit went off, collected seven other spirits, all more evil than itself, and they came back and took up residence there, so that the last state of the man was worse than the first. (Matthew 12:43-45).

❦

The story shows what a dangerous state emptiness is. We could have the most fertile garden in the world, but if we leave it empty, it will inevitably fill up with weeds.

If we have an empty garden we can plant things in it. If we have an empty house we can buy furniture for it. If we have an empty refrigerator we can buy food to put in it. But how do we fill an empty heart?

Some try to fill the void with possessions, only to discover that the emptiness increases with each new acquisition.

Others try to fill it with work. But when for any reason they are deprived of their work, the feelings of emptiness come rushing back in.

Others try to fill it through ill-chosen relationships, which bring them more pain than enrichment. Van Gogh took in a poor unfortunate woman, partly out of pity, and partly to fill the great void in his life. Needless to say, it didn't work.

Others try to fill it through the pursuit of pleasure, only to find that they have filled it with melancholy and self-disgust.

Others try to fill it through the pursuit of power, only to find themselves anguished and alone.

Others try to fill it through alcohol and/or drugs, only to find that they are sharing it with seven devils.

So what must we do? The most important thing is to make sure that we have love in our hearts. Without love the heart will always be empty. This means loving ourselves in the first place.

There is an idea that love of self is wrong, even sinful. There is a form of self-love which is wrong. We call it selfishness or egoism. But there is a form of self-love which is healthy and good, and without which we cannot love others properly. We can only love with the amount of love that is in us. Whether we are conscious of it or not, we love others precisely as we love ourselves.

Love starts at home, but it must not end there. We must reach out beyond ourselves. It is a good thing to love something, even a rose bush. If possible we ought to love all of God's creation.

But above all we need to share our love with people. We need wholesome friendships. To feel this need is not a sign of sickness but of health. 'It is not good for a human being to be alone' (Genesis 2:18).

Jesus himself felt the need for friendship and companionship. Throughout the exacting years of his public ministry he had the company of the apostles, whom he loved and who loved him. But he had other close friends. Among the latter were Martha, Mary, and Lazarus. When other doors were being closed against him, their door remained open to him.

However, Jesus knew the limitations of human friendships. On the last night he said to his apostles, 'The time will come – in fact it has already come – when you will be scattered, each going his own way and leaving me alone. And yet I am not alone, because the Father is with me' (John 16:32). From this we can see that what filled the heart of Jesus was his relationship with his heavenly Father. The person who is connected with God is never alone.

❦

But we have to face the fact that there is something missing in everybody's life. In every human heart there is an empty chamber waiting for a guest. Here on earth we never reach a stage where we are completely satisfied. Far from being a bad thing, this is a good and necessary thing. The satisfied person fails to develop further. This wanting has to be kept alive. We must take care lest it be stifled by too much having. It is worth more than any pleasure. It is this longing that draws us forward,

The emptiness which at times we all experience can be an opportunity for grace. The fact that we are empty, and admit it, means that God can fill us from his abundance. The apostle John was able to say: 'From his fullness we have all received' (John 1:16).

If that happens then our last state will be a thousand times better than our first.

So, if we sometimes become aware of a certain emptiness in our hearts we should not despair. A sense of something missing is God's way of calling us into greater intimacy with himself. It is God's way of hollowing out in us a space into which he can pour his love and his joy. 'It is grace that forms the void inside of us, and it is grace alone that can fill the void' (Simone Weil).

## The Hunger of the Heart

SINCE the dawn of time people have been looking for treasure. In olden times they looked for it in the fields, in the hills, under the ground. Today they are more likely to look for it in the lottery, the casino, the stock market. In one way or another, all of us are treasure-hunters in the sense that all of us are looking for happiness. There is nothing wrong with that. However, many search in vain.

Many seek happiness via money. If money could buy happiness then someone like Christina Onassis, daughter of billionaire shipping magnate, Aristotle Onassis, should have had a long and happy life. Yet she was only thirty-eight years of age when she died from the abuse of drugs. On the outside she had everything, on the inside she had nothing. If we do not find happiness within ourselves we won't find it elsewhere.

❦

Jesus understood the hunger for happiness that lies deep in the heart of every person. He liked searchers and had encouraging words for them. He said: 'Ask, and it will be given to you; seek, and you will find; knock, and the door will be opened to you' (Luke 11:9). But he had no such words for the smug and the satisfied. To these he said: 'Alas for you who have your fill now: you will go hungry' (Luke 6:21).

The first thing he tells us is where not to look for happiness. He says: 'Do not store up treasures for yourselves on earth, where moths and woodworms destroy and thieves break in and steal' (Matthew 6:19). He is telling us not to seek happiness in the things of this world. Of themselves these can never satisfy the human heart. They are only a means to an end.

Next he points us in the right direction. He says: 'Store up treasures for yourselves in heaven, where neither moth nor woodworms destroy them and thieves cannot break in and steal' (Matthew 6:20).

He goes on to say: 'Set your hearts on the Kingdom of God, and all these other things will be given you as well' (Matthew 6:33). Here he is telling us that we must really *want* the Kingdom. There is a difference between needing and wanting. The stomach needs; the heart wants.

He compared the Kingdom to a treasure hidden in a field. When someone finds the treasure, he gladly sells everything he owns and buys the field. Again he compared the Kingdom to a rare pearl. When a merchant finds such a pearl, he goes and sells everything he owns and buys it. (Matthew 13:44-46).

He is telling us that not only must we want the Kingdom, but we must want it more than anything else. The Kingdom must become our treasure. And he says, 'Where your treasure is, there will your heart be also' (Matthew 6:19-21). And where our heart is, there our happiness lies.

§

The Kingdom of God is a very simple concept. It means to know that we are children of God, with a divine dignity and an eternal destiny. When a sense of the presence of God, and a certainty about his love, suddenly bursts upon us, it is the most wonderful experience in the world. It brings peace to the mind, warmth to the heart, and joy to the spirit.

Those who taste the joy of the Kingdom have a different attitude to the things of this world. They know they still need a certain amount of them in order to live, but they no longer make them the be-all and the end-all of their lives. The richer one's inner life is, the simpler one's outer life becomes, and the less one needs or wants. There are more happy people to be found in conditions of hardship and self-sacrifice than in conditions of ease and luxury.

There have been many but futile attempts at producing an artificial happiness. Most of these have to do with satisfying our desires. It is folly to think that happiness comes from the fulfilment of our desires. One of the most beautiful discoveries in life is the discovery of how little we need to get by, and the extraordinary spiritual freedom and peace that brings.

> People rush about in express trains, but they do not know what they are looking for. They raise five thousand roses in the same garden, and still they do not find what they are looking for. Yet what they are looking for could be found in a single rose (Antoine de Saint Exupery, *The Little Prince*).

❦

From time to time all of us know moments of great joy and peace. In his goodness, God allows us to taste on earth the joys of the world to come. But it is a fragile happiness. Besides, fleeting moments of joy, no matter how wonderful, will never satisfy our heart. What we long for is unattainable here – a permanent state of happiness.

So what must we do? Like desert travellers, we must go forward from one oasis to another, with the conviction that God has a homeland prepared for us at the end of our journey. This conviction makes it possible for us to travel onwards with an ache in our heart and an unquenchable longing in our soul.

The pearl of great price is not an illusion. The Kingdom of God is that pearl. Only God can give us what we are looking for. In God all our scattered longings are gathered together. In the immortal words of St Augustine: 'You made us for yourself, O Lord, and our hearts will never rest until they rest in you.'

## The Testing of Hearts

The one essential thing one would expect to find in a religious person is, I believe, the virtue of compassion. Without a warm, compassionate heart one cannot call oneself a true human being, never mind a truly religious person.

❦

One day a lawyer came to Jesus and said to him, 'Teacher, which is the most important commandment of the Law?' And Jesus answered, 'You must love God with all your heart, with all your soul, with all your mind, and with all your strength. And the second is similar to this: You must love your neighbour as yourself.'

'Who is my neighbour?' the lawyer then asked. Instead of answering directly Jesus told him a story. It was about a man who was going down from Jerusalem to Jericho and who was attacked by robbers. The robbers beat him up and then left him lying by the side of the road, half dead.

A priest came on the scene. But instead of helping the wounded man he passed by on the other side of the road. Next a Levite came on the scene. (The Levites worked in the Temple as helpers to the priests). But he too passed by on the other side of the road.

Then a Samaritan came along. On seeing the wounded man, he was moved with compassion and administered first aid to him. Then he lifted him onto his donkey, took him to an inn, and had him taken care of at his own expense.

Turning to the lawyer Jesus asked, 'Which of the three acted like a true neighbour to the man who got beaten up?'

'The Samaritan, I guess,' the lawyer answered.

'Correct,' said Jesus. 'Now, go and do as he did.' (Luke 10:29-37).

❦

In order to appreciate the full thrust of Jesus' story we have to keep the following in mind. It is presumed that the man who got beaten up was a Jew. The two people who refused to help him were fellow

Jews and religious people to boot. The man who helped him was not a fellow Jew and probably not even a religious man. He was a Samaritan. At that time a centuries-old feud existed between the Jews and the Samaritans.

At the start of the story we know very little about the priest, the Levite, and the Samaritan. At the end of it we still don't know much about them. Yet we know all that matters. We know the kind of people they are because their hearts have been revealed to us.

How does Jesus accomplish this? Very simply. He places them in a situation. He brings them face to face with a man lying seriously wounded by the side of the road. They are faced with a decision: to stop and help him, or to ignore him and continue on about their own business. They have to commit themselves one way or another. The priest and the Levite decide to pass by; the Samaritan decides to stop and help.

Crisis does not create character, it merely reveals it. In times of crisis people reveal what is already inside them – the generous person or the selfish person, the hero or the coward. One moment or event can cause a person to reveal his essential being. The encounter with the wounded man was such a moment for the priest, the Levite, and the Samaritan.

❦

What did the incident reveal about the priest and the Levite? A very damning thing, namely, that they were cold-hearted individuals. To be cold-hearted is to be unable to show compassion. Cold-hearted people keep others at a distance. And while there may be great efficiency and dedication, there is no warmth. A cold-hearted person is like a fireplace without a fire.

From a spiritual point of view, one of the most damning things that can be said about anyone is that he/she has a cold heart. We are talking here about a permanent state, not a temporary state that most people flit in and out of.

To be hard-hearted is more serious still. It is to be unable to show pity or mercy. A hardening of the heart eventually leads to the death of the heart. It is only one step away from being heartless.

And to be heartless is to be indifferent, cruel, and ruthless. This was the situation with the robbers.

And what did it reveal about the Samaritan? A very admirable thing, namely, that he was a warm-hearted person. This means that he was capable of kindness, tenderness, compassion, pity and mercy. He was the kind of man who could not pass another human being in pain without wanting to relieve that pain. People like him restore our faith in the essential goodness of human beings.

The extent of our virtue is determined, not by what we do in extraordinary circumstances, but by our normal behaviour. It's clear that the goodness of the Samaritan was not a transitory thing but a permanent part of his being. And in all probability he wasn't even conscious of it. This is the highest state to which a person can attain.

How can we attain to this state? It cannot be achieved overnight. It has to be learned by long practice. It is achieved not by a few great deeds but by a lot of little ones. Every evil deed we do tends to harden our hearts and deaden them. Every good deed we do softens our hearts and brings them to life.

❧

Jesus' parable applies to us all because the road from Jerusalem to Jericho represents the road of life. We can't tell in advance what will happen to us on this road. But this much we can tell: our hearts will be tested on this road, and the hearts of others will be revealed to us.

When I look back over the road I have travelled I realise that sometimes I have been the wounded one in need of help. I have known that sinking feeling that grips you when people pass you by. But I have also known the warm feeling that takes hold of you when someone approaches you and utters those magic words, 'Can I help you?'

Other times I have been the one who came upon another in need of help. Alas, sometimes, like the priest and the Levite, I have passed by. I know the sadness that descends on one when that happens. But, thankfully, there have been times when I have acted like the Samaritan. I know the joy that wells up inside one when that happens. This is one's real reward, and it is more than enough.

## The Revelation of Hearts

THERE is no more compassionate and understanding person towards those who fall than the genuinely holy person. The holy person knows that good and evil are closely entwined. St Philip Neri, on seeing a man being led to the gallows, exclaimed, 'There but for the grace of God go I.' On the other hand, there is no more judgemental and condemnatory person than the self-righteous person. This explains in part why the Pharisees were so critical of Jesus.

Jesus adopted a sympathetic attitude towards sinners. He didn't just tolerate sinners; he welcomed them. He didn't wait for them to come to him; he sought them out. In associating with sinners he wasn't condoning their situation. Rather, he was trying to show them a better way. But he could not do this without associating with them. We never improve people by shunning them.

What really scandalised the Pharisees was the fact that Jesus did not wait for sinners to repent before befriending them. He befriended them *while they were still sinners*. They themselves would have nothing to do with sinners. They assumed that God had no dealings with them either. The central dogma of their religion was: 'God loves the virtuous, and hates the sinner.' In what is regarded as his greatest story Jesus showed them a very different kind of God.

❦

The story was about a man who had two sons. One day the younger son asked his father for his share of the estate. Having got it, he left for a foreign country. There he proceeded to blow his money on wild living. As long as the money lasted, he had no shortage of friends. But as soon as it the money was gone, he found himself alone. To make matters worse a famine occurred.

In desperation, he hired himself out to a farmer who put him minding pigs. (This shows how low he had sunk, because the Jews regarded pigs as unclean animals and would have nothing to do with them). At times he was so hungry that he ate some of the food the pigs got. This quickly brought him to his senses. So he decided to go back home and tell his father that he was sorry, in the hope that he would take him back, if not as a son, then at least as a hired servant.

The father saw him coming. (The implication is that he was on the look out for him.) Now given the fact that the son had betrayed him, and brought disgrace on the whole family, we would expect the father to put on a stern face and to keep his distance. Instead, what did he do? He ran out to meet him, threw his arms around him, and kissed him tenderly.

Then the son said, 'Father, I have sinned against heaven and against you. I no longer deserve to be called your son.' But the father made no reply. Instead he ordered the servants to get him some clean clothes, to put a ring on his finger and sandals on his feet. He told them to kill the calf they had been fattening, so that they could have a party to celebrate his son's home-coming. In no time the party got under way, and the house rang with music and laughter.

Towards evening the older son was coming back in from the fields after his day's work. Hearing the music, he asked a servant what the meaning of it was. The servant told him that his brother had come back, and his father had thrown a party for him.

On hearing this he flew into a rage, and wouldn't even go into the house. When the father came out to try to get him to come in, he let fly at him: 'I've stayed home all these years. I've worked my guts out for you, and what thanks do I get? Did you ever give a party for me? No. But when this hobo comes back, only the best is good enough for him! This waster who squandered your hard-earned money on wine and women.'

But the father said, 'Son, you have always been with me, and all

I have is yours. As regards the party for your brother, try to see it from my point of view. In spite of what he did, he's still my son. I just had to celebrate, because my son was dead, and has come back to life; he was lost, and has been found.' (Luke 15:11-32).

❦

You could say that the entire Gospel is contained in this story. Yet people react to it in different ways. Some think it is a fantastic story. Others think it is a very unfair story. Our reaction to the story will tell us much about the state of our own heart and the quality of our relationship with God.

Those who maintain that it is an unfair story feel sorry for the older son, convinced that he got a raw deal. They believe the younger son got away with murder. He should have been punished. He should have been taught a lesson.

The first thing that needs to be said is that the younger son behaved very badly. What he did was wrong, selfish, and irresponsible. He betrayed his family, his friends, himself, and the whole Jewish way of life. But he redeemed himself by coming back home and asking for forgiveness. The decision to come home was not an easy one. And the road back was a long one, not necessarily in miles, but long because of the burdens he was carrying.

It is easy to come back home when you are a hero, laden with trophies. But he was coming home empty-handed. He was a failure. Worse – he was a sinner. He was coming home laden with shame and disgrace. Furthermore, he knew that everything was out of his control. What would he do if his father didn't accept him back?

He deserved to be punished. He knew it and even asked for it. Yet punishment was the last thing he needed. To punish him would be like pouring water on a dying fire. In any case, he had already been punished. He had suffered loneliness, humiliation, degradation, and hunger. On top of all these, there was the remorse he felt at having betrayed his father's love. He did not need more punishment.

Nor did he need to be taught a lesson. He had already *learned* a lesson – something which is far more important. He had learnt some very painful truths about himself, about others, and about life. He had eaten forbidden fruit, and far from being satisfied, was left with a bitter taste in his mouth.

But what about the older son? Was he not a model son? Yes and no. Outwardly he was obedient and dutiful, but inwardly all was far from well with him. Inside him was a bitter heart. His service was motivated by a sense of duty rather than by love. Unless one is motivated by love, the performance of a duty can result in a withering of the heart.

In truth, he cut a sad figure. He was doing all the right things yet had no joy in his heart. He felt neglected and taken for granted. Instead of reaching out a welcoming hand to his brother, he turned inwards and grew resentful. Joy and resentment cannot coexist in the same heart.

❦

Essentially Jesus was telling the Pharisees three things.

The first concerned God: God is never happier than when welcoming back repentant sinners.

The second concerned himself: he had been sent to bring home the lost children of God.

The third concerned themselves: the older son was a mirror image of them. The problem with the older son was that he didn't see himself as a sinner. That was their problem too. If they saw themselves as sinners, they would have a more compassionate attitude towards sinners.

❦

In the story the hearts of the three main characters are laid bare.

The heart of the younger son is selfish and rebellious to begin with, but in the end it becomes repentant and loving. The heart of the older son is dutiful to begin with, but gradually it becomes bitter and resentful. And the heart of the father is revealed as constant. It never grows cold, or hard, or resentful, but remains open, warm, and forgiving towards both of his sons.

The hearts of the two sons show us the vagaries of the human heart. The human heart can be generous or selfish, open or closed, warm or cold, humble or proud, joyful or sad, repentant or unrepentant, forgiving or unforgiving, grateful or resentful.

The heart of the father shows us what the heart of God is like. God's heart does not blow hot and cold. God never closes his heart to any of his children.

The story doesn't give us a licence to sin. But it does show that if, through human weakness or wickedness, we do sin, then we can come back. Our past can be overcome. We can make a fresh start.

The only thing that truly heals people is unconditional love. It doesn't do us much good to be loved for being perfect. We need to be accepted and loved precisely as sinners. Only those who have experienced this kind of love can know what it is like. Being loved like this puts us in touch with our true nature, and to touch our true nature is to come home.

## The Proud Heart and the Humble Heart

ONE Sunday morning I was standing outside a church, chatting with people as they arrived for Mass. One man I got talking to launched forth: 'Isn't it terrible weather, Father? We've had no spring this year. I think the Man Above is giving us a message. The world is in a terrible state. There's nothing but robberies, murders, and rapes. How long more will the Lord put up with them? I think he'll bring about a purge soon.' At a certain point he glanced at his watch and said, 'Oh, I'd better go inside, or I'll be late for Mass.' A strange mentality with which to enter the house of God.

From a religious point of view, the man was clearly a very observant man. The danger people like that face is smugness. It is easy to grow complacent in our observances, and mistake them for the salvation that comes from God alone. When that happens we develop a 'them and us' mentality, something that is very dangerous. Firstly, it is a denial of our shared humanity. And secondly, it means we are in danger of constructing an image of God to fit our own prejudices.

❧

Jesus had a story for people like that. It was about two men who went into the Temple to pray. One was a Pharisee, the other a tax collector. The Pharisee went right up to the front, stood there where everyone could see him, and lifted up his eyes to God. He began by thanking God that he was not like other people. Other people were all thieves, rogues, and adulterers. He was a virtuous man. He fasted twice a week, and gave a tenth of his annual income for the support of the priests and the upkeep of the Temple.

Meanwhile, the tax collector too was praying. But he stayed down at the back, and wouldn't even lift his eyes to heaven. He just beat his breast and said, 'Lord, be merciful to me, a sinner.'

And Jesus concluded by saying, 'The tax collector went home at rights with God; the Pharisee did not. For those who exalt themselves will be humbled, while those who humble themselves will be exalted.' (Luke 18:9-14).

❧

The Pharisee was a very observant man. But, like the man outside the church, he succumbed to a very common temptation: the temptation to confess the sins of others rather than one's own. But his problem went deeper. He didn't believe he was a sinner at all. Therefore, he felt no need of God's mercy.

If the Pharisee had his way, the tax collector would not have been allowed into the Temple at all. Likewise there are people who believe that sinners have no place in church. If they had their way only saints would be admitted. But that would result in a very small church, and would make as little sense as a hospital that accepted only healthy people.

We go to church, not because we think we are saints, but because we know we are sinners. We are humble enough to admit our sinfulness, but brave enough to strive for something better.

When we enter a church we are conscious of coming before God. In the presence of God we become acutely aware of God's greatness and our insignificance. And we realise that whereas God is all-perfect, we are sinful creatures. How then can anyone come before God and dare to look down on anyone else?

❦

To cross the threshold of the house of God is to be humbled. Inside here entitlements count for nothing, and privilege is blown away like smoke before the wind. But when we let go of those things that give us a false sense of superiority, and which separate us from others, a beautiful thing happens. We find that we are exalted, just as Jesus said. We begin to realise our incredible greatness. Our greatness lies in the fact that we are children of God.

Before God all of us are equal. It is not that we are all reduced to the lowest common denominator. No. It is that we are all raised up. We are like people set on a mountain top. On a mountain top to speak of higher and lower places would be silly.

To enter a house of worship is to stand on holy ground. On approaching the burning bush Moses was told to take off his shoes. When we enter a house of worship we should rid our hearts of pride, and shed all attitudes of superiority. 'Humble yourselves before the Lord and he will lift you up' (James 4:10).

The Pharisee entered the Temple with a false sense of his own virtue, and left it in that same illusory state. The tax collector entered the Temple with a deep sense of his own sinfulness, and left it with a profound sense of the goodness of God.

It is good for us to be humbled from time to time. But there is something better – to humble ourselves. This is what the tax collector did. Humility is good for the soul. No one can attain to greatness in the spiritual life without first descending to lowliness. 'Humility like darkness reveals the heavenly lights' (Henry David Thoreau).

❦

We cannot pray properly unless the heart is right. The heart of the Pharisee was not right; it was full of pride, and full of himself. In effect, it was a closed heart. The heart of the tax collector was right; it was humble, open, and receptive.

We should heed the words of the psalmist: 'Who shall climb the mountain of the Lord? Who shall stand in his holy place? Those who cast no slur on their neighbours, but whose delight is in the law of the Lord. Such people will receive blessings from the Lord.' (From Psalms 24 and 15).

And we would do well to make our own the prayer of the tax collector: 'Lord, be merciful to me, a sinner.' If we sincerely pray that prayer, it will keep us in right relationship with God and with our fellow human beings. And it will enable us to grasp, with tranquil hearts, both our grandeur and our insignificance in the world.

## The Greedy Heart

A WOMAN who worked delivering meals-on-wheels in New York city told me how she came across elderly people, who had a million dollars in the bank, yet were living in poverty. You wonder why they didn't spend some of that money on themselves. More than likely it was because that money was their security. These were people who had come up through hard times. They knew what it meant to be without money. But no doubt greed also played a part in it.

Jesus told a story to warn us against greed, and to dispel the notion that security can be found in possessions.

❦

There was a rich farmer who grew wheat on his farm. One year, after a particularly good harvest, he said to himself, 'What am I to do? My barn is too small to hold all this wheat.' Then he said, 'I know what I'll do. I'll pull down the old barn and build a new and bigger one. When that is full, I'll say to my soul: My soul, you have plenty of wheat stored up for many years to come. Take things easy. Enjoy life.' But he never got to build that new barn. God said to him, 'You fool! This very night you're going to die, and you will have to leave it all behind.'

Jesus concluded by saying, 'So it is when people store up treasure for themselves instead of making themselves rich in the sight of God. Beware of greed. What good would it do you if you gained the whole world but lost your soul?' (Luke 12:16-21; 9:25).

❧

The farmer was searching for security. In biblical times famine was a recurrent threat. Hence, people sought security by stockpiling grain. In his search for security and happiness in this life, the farmer forgot God, eternal life, and his obligations to the poor. He was truly a 'fool' because he didn't know how to use wisely the wealth that he had.

But the farmer was also guilty of greed. His barn was full already, but he still wasn't satisfied. The dread of hunger when the granary is full is a hunger that can never be satisfied. He discovered too late that material wealth is not a permanent possession. All his plans and hopes burst like a bubble.

Because he devoted all his energy to amassing property, he had nothing he could call his own, and death revealed his essential poverty. The only possessions worth striving for are those which death cannot take away. 'When your last hour strikes, count only on what you have become' (Antoine de Saint Exupery).

❧

In our times people seek security by stockpiling money and/or possessions. People accumulate things and cling to them, because they give the illusion of security. The human search for security is an understandable one. But security cannot be found in possessions. Security can be found only in God. Jesus' parable stresses the foolishness of depending on material things for one's security rather than on God.

People of faith do not rely on material things but on God, who is everlasting love. God is their security, and their chief concern is to do his will. This gives them a deep trust in life, and enables them to live the present moment free from attachments and worries.

Greed is also a big danger in our times. One of the chief problems today is that people don't know when they are well-off. We have to learn to distinguish between *wants* and *needs.* Our wants are many but our needs are few. Food is an example of a need. If this is not met, we die of hunger. A television set is an example of a want. Having it contributes to our enjoyment, but we could live without it. Want can easily turn into greed.

Our aim should be to live simply. Living simply frees us to develop the spirit, and brings extraordinary spiritual freedom and peace. 'People don't know what they are striving for. They exhaust themselves in the senseless pursuit of material things, and die without realising their spiritual greatness' (Alexander Solzhenitsyn).

Besides, it is not how many possessions we have that matters, but how we enjoy the ones we have. Wealth is not in possession but in enjoyment. Many people have lost their capacity for enjoyment, especially those in affluent countries. They have to have more and more expensive gadgets, but are unable to enjoy the simple things of life.

❦

Life is fragile and fleeting. But it is this very fragility and fleeting-ness that makes it so precious. God wants us to live life. Jesus said, 'I came so that you may have life and have it to the full' (John 10:10). It ought to be possible to enjoy life to the fullest while being devout and religious at the same time. Life is generous to those who seize it with both hands. Those who live fully and intensely will not feel cheated at death. 'Fear not that your life will end; fear, rather, that it may never have begun' (Henry David Thoreau).

As well as security, people seek prestige and status in posses-sions. In our society people are estimated by what they have. To be considered a success you have to have certain symbols, such as a big house, a fancy car, and so on. But this is a false trail.

John Steinbeck wrote: 'It has always been strange to me, that the things that we admire in people – kindness, generosity, openness, honesty, understanding and feeling – are the concomitants of failure in our system. And those traits we detest – sharpness, greed, acquisitiveness, meanness, egotism and self-interest – are the traits of success.' (*Cannery Row*)

Jesus said that rather than storing up treasure for ourselves we should seek to make ourselves rich in the sight of God. What makes us rich in the sight of God is not what we *own*, but what we *are*. And how are we to measure what we are? By looking at the heart. We are what the heart is. The only riches worth accumulating are the riches of the heart. A noble and generous heart makes us rich in the sight of God.

❦

The damage done to the heart by a craving for security and by greed is incalculable. A craving for security prevents us from opening our heart to life, and living it fully and joyfully. It also makes us miserly towards others. 'No one is meaner than the one who is mean to himself' (Sirach 14:5).

The damage done to the heart by greed is even greater. Greed is like a fire – the more wood you pile on it, the hungrier it gets. A greedy heart cannot be happy because it is never satisfied. And by causing us to be totally focused on ourselves, greed blights our capacity for sharing.

We should seek to build the house of our lives on something solid. But how do we do this? By building it on the words of Jesus. The rain may come down, the floods may rise, gales may assail that house, but it will not fall because it is built on a rock. (Matthew 7:24-25).

## The Foolish Heart and the Wise Heart

WISDOM is one of the great themes of the Bible. This should come as no surprise. Without wisdom we are like travellers in the dark. With wisdom we have a lamp for our steps and a light for our path. However, the wisdom in question is not worldly wisdom. It is divine wisdom. Through wisdom God communicates to us the meaning of life, and the grandeur of our destiny, which is to be with God.

Wisdom is as much a matter of the heart as the head. Jesus urged his disciples not to allow themselves to get distracted but to keep their hearts focused on the Kingdom of Heaven. He told a story to illustrate the need for vigilance.

❦

The story was about ten bridesmaids who took their lamps and went to meet the bridegroom to accompany him to the wedding feast. Five of them were foolish and five were wise. The wise ones took extra oil with them. The foolish ones did not.

The bridegroom was late in coming, and they all grew drowsy and fell asleep. But at midnight a cry arose, 'The bridegroom is coming! Go out to meet him.' At this, all the bridesmaids woke up to discover that their lamps had gone out.

This was no problem for the wise bridesmaids. They simply refilled their lamps with the spare oil they had brought with them and then re-lit them. But it was a big problem for the foolish bridesmaids. They begged some oil from the wise ones. But they said, 'Sorry, we've barely got enough for ourselves. You had better go to the merchants and buy some.'

The foolish bridesmaids set off to buy oil. But while they were away the bridegroom arrived. The wise bridesmaids went in with him to the wedding feast and the door was closed. Sometime later the foolish bridesmaids arrived. They knocked on the door and cried, 'Lord, Lord, open the door for us.' But he replied, 'Go away, I do not know you.' (Matthew 25:1-13).

❦

It might seem that the Lord is being unduly hard on the foolish bridesmaids. It seems that they are denied access to the wedding feast just because they forgot to bring along some extra oil for their lamps. But it is not as simple as that. It is clear that we are not talking about a momentary lapse of memory on the part of the foolish bridesmaids, but about two contrasting attitudes to the wedding feast.

For the wise bridesmaids, to accompany the bridegroom to the wedding feast was their top priority. They had set their hearts on it, and took all necessary steps to ensure that they would not miss out on it.

For the foolish ones, going to the wedding feast was more like a bit of a lark. Their hearts weren't really set on it. This explains the casual approach they adopted to it. The result was that they found themselves locked out. It wasn't that they were evil. It was just that they were careless and foolish.

❦

However, the Gospel makes it clear that God continues to love us even when we live foolishly and forget who we are and where we are going. And we won't be judged on a momentary lapse, but on our life as a whole. Still, we have to be on our guard against complacency, disillusionment, foolishness, and distraction.

Jesus' parable is meant as a warning. This warning is itself a sign of his love for us. He wants to save us from the fate of arriving at heaven's door only for him to say to us: 'Go away, I do not know you.'

There is one way we can ensure that the Lord will recognise us when we arrive at the door to the heavenly kingdom. That is by keeping the lamp of love burning brightly. 'Everyone will know that you are my disciples by the love you have for one another' (John 13:35).

Wise disciples of Jesus will tend this lamp with special care. But how do we keep the lamp of love burning? Through a continuous input of small drops of oil. What do these drops of oil consist of? They are the small things of daily life, the little words and deeds of kindness and of service. These are the drops that keep the flame of love alive in our hearts.

## The Barren Heart

THERE are many activities which call for a lot of hard, patient, and sometimes frustrating work. Writing is an example. Writing would be easy if one could get it right at the first attempt. But it is not like that. One has to produce many drafts before something finally shapes up. That is how it is with life too. One may have to fail many times, make many mistakes, before, by the grace of God, one eventually gets it right.

Jesus understood the circumstances that can conspire to take people to places they never really wanted to be. He understood how the human heart, which holds such rich potential, can become barren. This led him to adopt a benign approach to sinners, something that brought him into conflict with the Pharisees. The Pharisees believed sinners should just be written off. Jesus didn't agree, and told them so in a story.

❦

The story was about a man who planted a fig tree in his vineyard. One day he came looking for fruit on the tree. Alas, there wasn't a fig to be found on it. So he said to the man who looked after the vineyard, 'For the past three years I have been coming to this tree in the hope of finding some figs on it, but I haven't found any. Cut it down. It's just taking up space.'

But the gardener replied, 'Sir, give it one more year. I'll dig round it, and manure it. It may bear fruit next year. If it doesn't, then you can cut it down.'

The man agreed. We are not told what happened to the fig tree, but it doesn't matter. Jesus had made his point. If a gardener can be patient with a fig tree, then surely God can be patient with sinners. (Luke 13:6-9).

❦

The attitude of the vineyard owner – Chop it down! It's contributing nothing! – seems eminently reasonable. But he was a businessman. He didn't care about the tree itself. He had done nothing for the tree. He had put nothing of himself into it. He was only interested in the end product – figs. Chopping it down was the easy option. It absolved him for doing anything to help the tree to become fruitful.

The gardener, on the other hand, was a tender of fruit trees. Better still, he was a lover of fruit trees. He cared about this little tree. He had sacrificed himself for the tree. The sacrifices he had made on its behalf enhanced its value in his eyes. A thing becomes precious to us, not so much because of what we get out of it, but because of what we've put into it. 'What nourishes the heart is not what one gets from the wheat, but what one gives to the wheat' (Antoine de Saint Exupery).

The gardener also knew about fig trees. He knew that it can take a lot of careful tending for a particular tree to become fruitful. If a fig tree was barren, he didn't give up on it. He tried to help it, by enhancing the soil, for example. And he was willing to wait for the harvest to come when the tree was ready.

The owner's way may have seemed sensible, but it was the way of the head rather than of the heart. It was the way of power rather than love. Power is only interested in results, and often wants them instantly. Power has no patience with the slow, no sympathy for the weak.

The gardener's way was the way of love. Love is patient and kind. Love doesn't give up easily. Love is always ready to endure, to trust, and to hope. Love doesn't force; it coaxes, encourages, and waits. The essence of love is to labour for something. Love and labour are inseparable. One loves that for which one labours, and one labours for that which one loves.

Jesus' way was the way of love. Whereas the Pharisees did nothing for sinners, he spent himself for sinners. He saw that they needed someone to take an interest in them, and to show them the way to something better. Many sinners responded to his love with the result that their barren lives became fruitful.

❦

The parable has many applications for our day. It originally addressed the problem of sinners in the Kingdom. However, by the time Luke recorded it in his Gospel, it served another purpose. It was meant to give encouragement to the early disciples. It was telling them to be patient, to trust, and not to expect instant results. This is a message that disciples of any time could take heart from.

It has been called the parable of the second chance. Sometimes we are not willing to give people a second chance. We tend to be harsh on others until we need a second chance ourselves. It doesn't help that we live in an unforgiving society. The attitude to criminals is: lock them up and throw the key away. Here there is no help, no forgiveness for errors, no allowance for the possibility of change. A society that doesn't believe in redemption is a society without hope.

For the owner of the vineyard results alone mattered. In his eyes the fig tree was a failure. We live in a world in which results are the only things that matter. Prizes are given for results, never for effort. Hence, some of our finest attributes often go unrewarded, attributes such as generosity, courage, and spirit. To judge by results alone is profoundly unfair. It is possible to do one's best and still have nothing to show for it at the end of the day.

But the original message of the parable is still relevant, and always will be, namely, that God is patient with us sinners. The history of the Church is full of examples of 'fig trees' which were once barren but which in time became fruitful. Some of the greatest names in the Church's register of saints fall into this category: Paul of Tarsus, Augustine of Hippo, Francis of Assisi, Ignatius of Loyola – to mention only a few.

Looking at the way Jesus dealt with sinners makes it easier for us to confront our own inadequacies. The Gospel offers hope to those who fail. Through God's goodness and mercy, our mistakes, our fumblings, yes, even our sins, become part the process that leads to fruitfulness.

# The Impoverished Heart

W HEN we think of poverty, we tend to think only of material poverty. But there is a worse kind of poverty – the poverty of living with a shrunken heart.

❦

Jesus told a story about a rich man (Dives), who used to dress in purple and fine linen and feast magnificently every day. Now at his gate lay a poor man by the name of Lazarus, who was covered with sores. Lazarus longed to fill himself with the scraps that fell from the table of Dives, but he didn't get them. His only comfort was provided by the street dogs, who from time to time came and licked his sores. Lazarus died and was carried away by angels to the bosom of Abraham. Dives died and was buried in Hades. (For full version, see Luke 16:19-31).

❦

Dives and Lazarus lived in different worlds. Dives was dressed in purple robes; Lazarus was dressed in rags. Dives ate splendidly every day; Lazarus didn't eat at all. Dives was healthy; Lazarus was covered with sores. Dives lived in a palace; Lazarus lived in the streets.

In fact, to say that they lived in different worlds would be an understatement. They lived in opposite worlds. Dives lived in a garden; Lazarus lived in a desert. Dives was in an earthly paradise; Lazarus in an earthly hell. And yet, though their respective worlds were as different as day and night, they lay side by side.

Dives could easily have entered Lazarus' lonely, desperate world, and made contact with him. But he didn't. He shut him out of his palace and out of his heart. He failed to see him as a fellow human being, much less a brother with whom he shared a common humanity.

Lazarus was about as poor as any man could be. Yet, in a sense, Dives was even poorer. How could that be? Lazarus was suffering from material poverty. Dives was suffering from poverty of heart.

His heart was devoid of compassion and love. Even the street dogs had more compassion than he. 'Without a rich heart, wealth is an ugly beggar' (Ralph Waldo Emerson). A person like Dives would be poor even if he owned the whole world.

Dives was condemned, not because he was rich, but because he didn't show compassion to the poor man. Sin is not just about doing wrong. It is also about not doing good. One of the greatest evils in the world is indifference towards one's neighbour.

While Lazarus was taken by angels to the bosom of Abraham, that is, to Paradise, Dives was buried in Hades. (*Hades* was the abode of the dead, also known as *Sheol*. Here it is portrayed as a place of exclusion and punishment.) It wasn't God who excluded Dives. He excluded himself – by shutting his heart against his brother. When he died his heart was closed forever. That's what hell means.

❦

Today we call people like Lazarus 'down-and-outs'. From time to time all of us encounter people like that. I think it is true to say that most of us find such encounters disturbing and humbling experiences. Why is this?

They are disturbing because they arouse within us conflicting feelings of pity, discomfort, anger, and guilt. They are humbling because they make us realise that we too are poor, only in a different way. Down-and-outs are poor materially. We are poor in compassion, poor in our willingness to help, poor in our capacity to love. In other words, poor at heart.

But such encounters can also be a blessing. They can act as a reminder to us that before God all of us are poor. They can awaken within us feelings of tenderness and compassion. Thus they can bring our heart to life, and enable us to enter the world of the poor and the excluded. 'What we avert our eyes from today can be borne tomorrow when we have learned a little more about love' (Dorothy Day).

The only riches that are worth having are the riches of the heart. Jesus compared the heart to a storehouse (Luke 6:45). If we wish to know how wealthy we are, let us not waste our time counting our possessions, or looking into our bank account. Let us look rather into the storehouse of our heart. 'Do you want to know what real poverty is?' asks Jerome Fleishman. 'It is never having a big thought or a generous impulse.'

## The Forgiving Heart

NONE of us can go through life without being hurt by other people. Fortunately most of the hurts we suffer are of a minor nature, and we recover quickly. But when a deep injury is done to us we never recover until we forgive.

❦

One day Peter asked Jesus, 'If someone offends me, how many times am I supposed to forgive him? Would seven times be about the limit?'

'No,' Jesus replied. 'Nor would seventy times seven times.' And he went on to tell a story about a king who called in all those who owed him money. One man came in who owed a very large sum of money. But when he pleaded to be given time, the king took pity on him and cancelled the entire debt.

Now on the way out, the man met a fellow servant who owed him a tiny sum of money. And guess what? He seized him by the throat and began to throttle him, saying, 'Pay what you owe me.' The poor man pleaded with him. But he wouldn't listen. He had him thrown into prison until he should pay the debt.

The king heard about this and immediately sent for the man. 'You wicked servant!' he said. 'I cancelled the big debt you owed me. Could you then not have cancelled the small debt that man owed you?'

The man hadn't a word to say for himself, and there was no point in putting on the begging act a second time. The king had him thrown into jail, until he paid back the sum he owed down to the last cent.

And Jesus concluded, 'That is how God will deal with you unless you forgive your brother from your heart.' (Matthew 18:23-3.

❧

There is no point in being glib about forgiveness. Forgiveness is never easy. The memory of wrongs done to us seeps into our heart, producing a legacy of bitterness, and destroying our capacity to love.

It is precisely the heart that is wounded. Forgiveness is the healing of our own heart. Unless we forgive, the heart can't heal. This is what makes forgiveness so necessary. A poison invades the hearts of those who cannot forgive; a balm invades the hearts of those who can.

To forgive is, first and foremost, a duty we owe ourselves. We forgive for the sake of our own well-being. We forgive because we don't want to live with feelings of resentment and desire for revenge. We forgive in order to cleanse ourselves of these poisonous attitudes and states of mind, so that we may be able to devote all our energies to loving, which is the only activity that befits a Christian.

One of the things that can motivate us to forgive is an appreciation of our own need of forgiveness. Jesus says that unless we forgive others God won't forgive us. The fault is not with God but with us. When we refuse to forgive others, we make it impossible for ourselves to receive God's forgiveness.

Imagine two people living in the same room. One of them closes the blind because he doesn't want the other to enjoy the sunlight. But in so doing he also deprives himself of the sunlight. To use another analogy: when we refuse to forgive we break down the bridge over which we ourselves must pass.

When we forgive, we ourselves are the main beneficiaries. But forgiveness also benefits the person who is forgiven. It sets the person free to walk in friendship with God and with the person he/she has offended. That is something we should sincerely desire to see happen.

❦

Jesus says that not only must we forgive, but we must forgive *from the heart*. For forgiveness to be effective it must be sincere and warm. A cold forgiveness is not much use. This is why forgiveness has to come from the heart.

Jesus also says that we must forgive 'seventy times seven times'. In other words, forgiveness must be unlimited. And it is not a question of forgiving if and when the offender repents – that would be relatively easy. We are expected to forgive even if the offender doesn't repent.

Forgiveness cannot be accomplished in a moment. It is not an event but *a process*. A process takes time. But at some point we have to make a decision to forgive. This doesn't mean that feelings of hurt and bitterness will suddenly disappear. The healing of these feelings will take time.

We constantly fall short of complete forgiveness. Perhaps that is why Jesus tells us that we have to forgive seventy times seven. There is no moment when we do not need forgiveness, and no moment when we do not need to be forgiving.

Forgiveness doesn't mean forgetting the wrong done to us. It means remembering and letting go. Forgiveness should start now. Putting it off only deepens the wound, prolongs bitterness, and postpones happiness. Forgiveness is one of the highest and most beautiful forms of love. It is a holy task. Only God can help us to accomplish it fully.

❦

One of the greatest prayers of forgiveness ever written, was found on a piece of paper in Auschwitz concentration camp. It goes like this:

'Lord, remember not only people of good will but also people of ill will. Do not remember only the sufferings that have been inflicted on us, but remember too the fruit we have bought as a result of this suffering: the comradeship and loyalty, the humility and courage, the generosity and greatness of heart that has grown out of it. And when they come to judgment, let all the fruits that we have borne be their forgiveness.'

## The Generous Heart

ONCE while travelling in a hearse to officiate at a burial service I had quite a chat with the driver. He told me with pride how he had risen from poverty to relative wealth. But he had had his troubles along the way. He had fallen victim to alcoholism but was now in recovery. He had buried a twelve year-old daughter. Even so, he was able to say that God had been good to him.

I warmed to him. It was clear to me that he was a good man, and a spiritual one too. Yet there was something about him that saddened me. It was his attitude to the poor. I would have expected that, as one who had once shared their lot, he would be understanding and compassionate towards them. Instead, he was harsh and judgmental. He resented any help given to them, seeing it as a betrayal of people like himself who had worked their way up without receiving help from anyone.

Sadly, such an attitude is not uncommon. There are those who can't bear to see others get things easier than themselves. According to this mentality you get what you earn. If you haven't earned anything, then you don't deserve to get anything. In this kind of world there is no room for grace. Grace is favour extended to undeserving people as a gift.

Jesus encountered a similar mentality. He met religious people who begrudged his kindness to sinners. In their eyes he was betraying the virtuous. They assumed that God works on the merit system. According to this system, you must earn your graces by hard work. Jesus didn't agree with them.

💝

He told a story was about a man who needed workers for his vineyard. He went out to the market-place at six o'clock in the morning, and found some people gathered there looking for work. They agreed to work for him for a denarius a day, the going rate. He went out again at nine o'clock, at noon and three o'clock in the afternoon, and took on more workers on the same terms. Finally he went out at five o'clock, and found people standing there. He took pity on them and brought them into his vineyard.

At the end of the day he surprised everyone by giving them all a denarius each. Even more surprising was the fact that he started the pay-out with the late-comers. On seeing this the early-comers complained bitterly, saying, 'This isn't fair. We've worked all day long in the burning sun. Those late-comers have done only an hour's work. Yet you have given them the same amount of money as you gave us.'

But the owner said, 'I'm not being unfair. Didn't you agree to work for a denarius? And haven't you got a denarius? So what are you complaining about? Are you envious because I am generous?'

And Jesus concluded, 'In the Kingdom of Heaven, the last will be first, and the first will be last.' (Matthew 20: 1-16).

❦

The eleventh-hour people were not idlers. They wanted to work. It was just that nobody had hired them. In effect, they were rejects. The idea that any employer would take such people on at the eleventh hour, and pay them a full day's wage, was unthinkable. Yet that is exactly what the owner of the vineyard did. This is the strong point of the parable.

Jesus is telling us that God does not work on the merit system. Where God is concerned we should never expect anything as a right. We can't put God in our debt. Hence, when we come into the presence of God, we shouldn't parade our entitlements, rights, and deserts.

❦

The story makes little sense from the point of view of strict justice. Justice is a very important thing. To realise how important it is all we have to do is think of its opposite. Anyone who has had the experience of being treated unjustly will know what a deep hurt it can cause. The story goes out of its way to stress that no injustice has been done.

Justice is to society what leaven is to bread. But the story is not about justice. Thank heavens for that. Which of us would like to be treated by God according to strict justice? Do we not all stand more in need of God's mercy than of God's justice?

The story is about generosity. Justice is a great thing, but it hasn't the sweetness of generosity. Generosity touches the heart in a way justice never does. However, the parable is not about human generosity, but about the generosity of God.

God's generosity utterly transcends human generosity. 'My thoughts are not your thoughts, nor are my ways your ways. As high as the heavens are above the earth, so high are my ways above your ways, my thoughts above your thoughts,' says the Lord (Isaiah 55:6-9).

God's generosity is a great comfort to us, but it is also a great challenge. If we have experienced that generosity in our own lives, far from begrudging it to others, we will try to imitate it in our dealings with others.

## Beatitudes of the Heart

Blessed are the open-hearted;
they will know what it is to be alive.

Blessed are the warm-hearted;
they will radiate goodness.

Blessed are the soft-hearted;
their lives will be fruitful.

Blessed are those who set their hearts on the Kingdom of God, everything else will be given to them.

But alas for those whose hearts are closed;
they will neither be able to give nor to receive.

Alas for those whose hearts are cold;
they will never know the warmth of true friendship.

Alas for those whose hearts are hard;
their lives will be barren.

Alas for those whose hearts are empty;
all the goods in the world will not satisfy them.

PART FOUR

# *Living from the Heart*

# Winter in the Heart

F EW people enjoy winter. Winter makes the world a cold and inhospitable place. It causes soft things to become hard, and turns the most fertile ground into a wasteland. It squeezes the life and joy out of everything. It seems that life has stopped, and we are not so much living as enduring. Winter would be intolerable but for the expectation of spring.

❦

Winter can take possession of the human heart too with equally devastating consequences. As we grow old we lose the fire, the energy, the idealism, and enthusiasm of youth. We also experience a lot of losses and disappointments. All of these take their toll on our resources, especially on our heart. As a result, the heart may grow cold and hard. Even the most generous heart can gradually harden and eventually freeze over.

However, nobody grows old merely by living a number of years. 'People grow old by deserting their ideals. We are as young as our faith, as old as our doubt; as young as our hope, as old as our despair. So long as our heart receives messages of beauty, cheer, courage, grandeur and power, so long are we young. But when the heart is covered with the snow of pessimism and the ice of cynicism, then we have gown old indeed, and may the Lord have mercy on our souls' (General Douglas MacArthur).

It would be a tragedy to reach old age with little joy or gratitude, and have to live with ourselves in hardness and bitterness of heart. We would be dying before our time. It has been said that hardening of the heart makes a person grow old faster than hardening of the arteries.

❦

A hard heart could be compared to an old wineskin. You can't put new wine into an old wineskin. New wine is still fermenting. As it ferments, it gives off gases, and therefore needs room to expand. If you put new wine into an old wineskin, the skin will burst, because it has become dry and hard, and so has lost the capacity to expand. A new wineskin, on the other hand, can receive new wine, because it has a certain elasticity in it that allows it to expand.

A hard heart gives a person a measure of invulnerability in so far as one can't feel, and therefore can't be hurt. But to adopt a hard-hearted attitude is to maim oneself. A hard heart can't experience sorrow, but neither can it experience joy. A hard heart is a closed heart, so it can't receive. A hard heart is a barren heart. From a spiritual point of view, hardness of heart is one of the worst things that can happen to anyone.

A soft heart, on the other hand, is a blessing. True, it makes a person vulnerable; the soft-hearted are easily hurt. But a soft heart can be touched, moved, and warmed. It can receive. It can be saddened, but can also be deliriously happy. It can respond. It can burst into life like a garden in springtime.

❦

How do we keep the heart soft, and thus keep it alive? By ensuring that we do not lose love, or the capacity to love. As long as we can give and receive love, the heart will stay soft. A soft heart will keep winter at bay, and save us from the death before death.

## Springtime in the Heart

SPRING is most people's favourite season, and it's easy to see why. Ice and snow melt, causing limpid streams to flow. The ground softens, allowing the flowers to emerge from their subterranean hiding places. The air warms up, enabling buds to burst open. The earth discards its winter rags and dons a bright new robe of many colours. In short, the world is turned from a wasteland into a wonderland.

Yet for all that, spring doesn't *make* anything happen. It merely creates a climate in which things can express themselves. The new life cannot be imposed; it has to come from within. What spring does is give living things the impulse to realise what is already inside them in a germinal state.

Spring's task is to awaken and call forth. This calling forth is a gentle process. Force is out of the question. Persuasion is the only effective weapon. Unless there is a response from within, all spring's efforts will be in vain.

❧

We too need to express ourselves. Expression is to us what leaf and blossom are to a tree. All of us have a capacity for goodness. Unless we express ourselves we cannot realise that capacity or fulfil ourselves. To express ourselves is the way to make ourselves whole. But expression cannot be imposed on us. If this is attempted it will merely result in an outward show. It will not enrich us, and will eventually wear out like a garment.

Some of us may have had violence done to us when we were young. People may have tried to press us into shape from the outside, or squeeze us into a mould, as if we were lumps of clay. That approach is counterproductive. What we need is someone to awaken us to what is inside us, to bid us live, and help us grow. In short, we need spring to come to us.

Spring comes when we open our heart. However, to open our heart is to become vulnerable. Hence, we may be tempted to construct a shell around our heart to protect the spot where we are most vulnerable. While this is understandable it is detrimental to growth. For growth to happen we must allow that protective shell to be broken and risk living with an unprotected heart.

We should learn from the buds. Initially they are wrapped up in a sheath to protect them from the cold. But gradually, under the influence of the sun, that sheath relaxes its embrace, allowing the buds to expand. Eventually the sheath disintegrates, and the buds are able to emerge.

Jesus said: 'I came that you may have life, and have it to the full' (John 10:10). The Chilean poet, Pablo Neruda, said something similar: 'I want to do with you what spring does with the cherry trees.'

Mere existence is not enough for us. We are meant to live. To open our heart is to begin to live. Anything, therefore, that helps us to open our heart enables us to live more fully. This will result in some pain. But there is a worse kind of pain – to live with a closed heart. Too many people are left with unopened hearts, and die without having experienced even one spring. Nevertheless, we shouldn't give up on anyone.

❦

Once, as I was passing an old cherry tree in January, I noticed that it had a bare and forlorn look about it. It contained not a shred of beauty. In fact, it required no small act of faith to believe that it was still alive.

I passed the tree again in April. When I looked at it now I could scarcely believe my eyes, so great was the transformation it had undergone in that short interval of time. It was now decked out in a robe of brilliant blossoms. Two months ago it looked like a corpse; now it was an eloquent witness to life.

'From where has all this beauty come?' I asked myself. Could it by chance have fallen out of the sky and landed on the tree? Or had someone waved a magic wand over the tree? Nothing of the kind.

All this newness, freshness and fragrance; all these buds, blossoms and shoots had come from within the tree itself! On looking at it back in January, when it was still in the grip of winter, who could have believed that it contained all this?

Sometimes on the evidence of just one encounter we write off people as having no possibilities. We do those people a grave injustice. Every human being is a well of possibilities. If in some people these possibilities have not yet manifested themselves, all it means is that for them spring has not yet come.

# Gentle and Humble of Heart

HUMILITY and gentleness are two beautiful virtues, but they don't seem to make much sense in today's world. There is a belief that if you are gentle, people will walk all over you. If you want to get to the top in any field of endeavour, but especially in business and politics, you have to be hard, even ruthless. Great leaders are known to have a ruthless streak.

As for humility, there would seem to be even less place for this in today's competitive world. We are told that if we want to get places we must assert ourselves.

Yet Jesus says, 'Learn from me, for I am gentle and humble in heart, and you will find rest for your souls' (Matthew 11:29).

❦

The problem with gentleness is that it tends to be equated with weakness. But gentleness is not a form of weakness. It is a form of strength. Nothing is so strong as gentleness, and noting so gentle as real strength. It takes a strong, self-confident person to be gentle.

Gentleness is one of the most necessary qualities in life. Think of the gentleness required in the hands of a mother or a surgeon. Deep down we all pine for gentleness, and can't open up and grow without it.

It is true that gentleness makes one vulnerable. But gentleness is one of the most irresistible human qualities and can penetrate even the hardest of hearts. Whereas harshness arouses resistance, gentleness causes resistance to crumble. If you love, you are gentle. And there are certain tasks that only gentleness can accomplish.

Jesus' approach to people was very gentle. He didn't impose his will on people. He respected their freedom. He invited rather than commanded. He didn't manipulate or oppress anyone. He sought to influence people rather than to control them. He carried no weapons, yet he could do what Stalin could never do – he could change people's hearts.

He was especially gentle towards the weak and the wounded. He would not break the crushed reed, or extinguish the smouldering wick (Matthew 12:20). He would have agreed with the sentiments expressed by the poet, William Butler Yeats:

> But I, being poor, have only my dreams;
> I have spread my dreams under your feet;
> Tread softly because you tread on my dreams.

The need for gentleness could hardly be expressed more beautifully. A gentle person knows that growth results not from forcing but from nurturing. 'A gentle person treads lightly, listens carefully, looks tenderly, and touches with reverence' (Henri Nouwen).

Jesus was gentle, but this doesn't mean that he was weak. When the occasion demanded it he could be very assertive – as when he drove the traders out of the Temple (John 2:13-22). But he did not lust after power. The lust for power is rooted in weakness. Only the weak measure their worth by the number of people they can dominate. Weaklings puff themselves up and try to act strong; tough people hide their vulnerabilities.

And Jesus was humble. Like gentleness, humility is a misunderstood virtue. True humility does not mean that we have to demean ourselves. It means that we recognise our true greatness, while acknowledging from Whom it comes. Like gentleness, humility is not a form of weakness. It is a from of strength. Besides, humility is the soil in which all other virtues flourish. There can be no true spirituality without humility.

❦

Those who are proud and insensitive make life burdensome for themselves and others. Those who are humble and gentle make life less burdensome for themselves and others.

To the gentle and humble Jesus promises peace of soul. If we were more gentle in our dealings with one another, we would have more peace in our homes and in the world. And if we were more humble, we would have more peace within ourselves and with others. Humble people disarm others. Gentle people bring out the best in them.

We could learn a lesson from nature. When the rain comes in the form of a downpour, it runs away quickly, often taking precious soil with it. But when it falls slowly and softly, it sinks into the ground, allowing growing things to drink it in. When the sun comes as a scorching heat, it causes growing things to shrivel up. But when it comes as a gentle warmth, it embraces and nurtures growing things. When the wind comes in the form of a storm, it damages everything in its path. But when it comes in the form of a breeze, it refreshes and enlivens everything it touches.

## The Lightening of Burdens

I T IS rare to get snow in late April in Ireland. One April morning a few years ago I went out for an early morning walk and was surprised to see that two inches of snow had fallen during the night. Since it had been a calm night, the snow rested where it fell. Some old rose bushes grow along the driveway. Normally they stand upright and you hardly notice them. But this morning you couldn't fail to notice them. Laden with snow, they were leaning out into the driveway. Some branches were so heavily laden that they were bent down almost to the ground.

Their leaves and swelling buds had provided a platform for the snow to rest on. Of course the more they listed, the more the snow piled up on them. So pitiable was their state, that one wondered if they would ever be able to straighten up again. But they still had one thing going for them. They hadn't snapped under the load. Their stems were unbroken.

On reaching the park I set out on my familiar round, completely forgetting the rose bushes. But when I got back to the driveway I witnessed a small miracle. The branches were beginning to lift their heads and straighten themselves up once more.

The explanation was simple. In the meantime, the sun had come up and was shining warmly on everything. Its warmth caused the snow to melt, and slowly but surely was ridding the branches of their burdens. Later in the day I noticed that the branches had resumed their old, upright stance. I was delighted because it meant they would bear another crop of roses.

❦

During the thirty years that Jesus spent at Nazareth he lived among the ordinary people. He lived the life of a working man. He knew at first-hand the difficulties and frustrations ordinary people had to contend with. He was aware of the heavy burdens life placed on their shoulders. Consequently, he had sympathy for the ordinary people and desired to lighten their burdens.

One of the things he said during his public ministry was: 'Come to me, all you who labour and are overburdened, and I will give you rest' (Matthew 11: 28). These are among the loveliest words in the Gospel.

Many people accepted his invitation. They came to him from all quarters with their burdens of sickness and misery. And all of them had their burdens lightened as a result of meeting him. Such was the charm of his personality that his mere presence could bring peace to an anguished soul.

Regarding his own burden he said, 'My yoke is easy and my burden is light.' How could he, who took on himself the burdens of so many, say that? Because he carried his burden with love.

Two people may be carrying the exact same burden. For one it is a crucifixion; the other takes it in his stride. Why the difference? The first person is forced to carry the burden; the second has chosen to carry it. While the first seems to have a very limited supply of energy available to him, the second seems to have a bottomless well of it.

There is a proverb which says: 'Some people are like the donkey that carries sandalwood: they know the burden, but not the fragrance.' But there are others who know the fragrance, but not the burden. They are the ones who bear their burden with love. Love makes a burden light and a sacrifice sweet.

❧

Religion should not make life more burdensome. Quite the opposite. If Jesus placed any burden on us, it was that of loving one another. But in exhorting us to open our hearts to others, he is not laying a burden on us. He is calling us to life, for to open our heart is to begin to live, whereas to close our heart is to begin to die.

Let us not be afraid then to come to the Lord. Let us sit in his presence as in the shade of a tree. Let us refresh ourselves here as at a running stream. Here we will find rest. Here we will find peace. And our yoke will become easy, and our burden light.

## Keeping the Heart Free of Hatred

NELSON Mandela spent some twenty-seven years in South African prisons. When he was finally released, people expected him to be full of hatred for the leaders of the white regime who had kept him in prison all those years. But what happened? He came out without a trace of hatred. In fact, he came out smiling, and immediately sought reconciliation with his former enemies. And sooner than anyone could have imagined, and peacefully, a multi-racial society came into being in South Africa. More marvellous still, Mandela himself became the first president of the new South Africa.

Mandela didn't turn on the charm just for the occasion of his release. This was how he had lived while in prison. He would not allow anyone to make him hate. If he hated anything it was the iniquitous system of apartheid. But he refused to hate the people who enforced that system. He knew how destructive hatred is. Hatred drives out everything else, and creates a legacy of bitterness and hostility.

Another man who understood this truth very well was Oscar

Wilde. When he was sent to prison it was a terrible humiliation for him. But while there he made a decision that he would not come out filled with hatred: 'Had I not a friend left in the world; were there not a single house open to me in pity; had I to accept the ragged cloak of sheer penury: as long as I am free from resentment, hardness, and scorn, I would be able to face life with much more calm and confidence than I would were my body clothed in purple and fine linen, and the soul within me sick with hate.' (*De Profundis*)

❦

Jesus said, 'In the old days you were told: Love your friends, and hate your enemies. But I say to you: Love your enemies, and pray for those who persecute you' (Matthew 5:43-44).

Love our enemies! We find it hard enough to love our friends, so how can we be expected to love our enemies? The enemy is not necessarily an enemy as in a war situation. The enemy is the person in our family, our community, our neighbourhood, our work-place, who in some way makes life difficult for us. Our enemies are not those who hate us but those whom we hate.

Enemies bring out the worst in us. They cause ugly things to rise up inside us. They expose a side of us which we usually manage to keep hidden from our friends, a dark side of our nature which we would rather not know about.. When we discover our capacity to hate and harm, it is very humiliating.

If the enemy arouses hatred within us he has done us terrible harm. When we hate we expend more energy than in any other emotion. This is why Jesus urges us not to have hatred in our hearts for anyone, not even our enemies. It is not only for the sake of the enemy that he says to us, 'Love your enemies', but for our own sake too. Hatred may not destroy its object but it will surely destroy the one who hates. 'Ten enemies cannot hurt a man as much as he hurts himself' (Yiddish Proverb).

We must not dissipate our strength in hating but save it for better things. Our hearts were made to love, not to hate. Love is more beautiful than hate. Hate poisons the heart, but love purifies it. At all costs, then, we must keep love in our heart. 'Better a dish of herbs when love is there than a fattened ox and hatred to go with it' (Proverbs 15:17).

❧

The teaching of Jesus may be difficult but it makes great sense. The escalation of evil can be stopped only by one who humbly absorbs it, without passing it on. Revenge and retaliation only add darkness to darkness. Revenge may satisfy a person's rage but it leaves the heart empty.

Jesus challenges us to respond to darkness with light. To respond to what is worst in the other with what is best in us. Most of us think we have done our Christian duty if we refrain from doing harm to our enemy. But Jesus asks more of us. He asks us to love our enemies. The way he proposes is not a soft way. It is a hard way, but it is a better way.

The image of God is at its best and brightest in us when we love. Love releases extraordinary energies in us. And love is never lost. If not reciprocated, it will flow back and soften and purify the heart.

## Getting the Heart Right

IN OUR culture the image is everything. Appearances are more important than the substance. But appearances can be deceptive. A nut may have a large shell, and yet be empty inside. You can't tell from the outside what is inside. But even a child knows that it is what is inside that matters.

❧

Israel needed a new king. The first king, Saul, on whom such great hopes and expectations had been placed, had proved a failure and been rejected by God. The prophet Samuel was commissioned by God to look for a new king.

Samuel's search led him to Bethlehem and to the household of

Jesse. There, one by one, he was introduced to seven of Jesse's sons. Judged by appearances, they had a lot going for them. They were tall, strong, and good-looking. Samuel was impressed. Yet he was not quite satisfied. Something told him to continue the search.

A wise and perceptive man, he wasn't going to judge by appearances. He knew that everything that makes up the kernel of a person is hidden from us. He was looking for something else, something not so obvious but which he felt he would recognise if and when he saw it.

Then, almost as an afterthought, the last of Jesse's sons was introduced to him. His name was David. Outwardly, he didn't have much going for him. He was a mere youth, still physically underdeveloped. But he did have something going for him. He had 'fine eyes and a pleasant bearing'. To Samuel this indicated a good heart.

He knew then that his search for a successor to Saul was over. He anointed David straightaway. And God approved of his choice. In spite of failures and weaknesses, David made a good king, and is one of the most important figures in the Old Testament.

The great lesson of this story is that while we look at appearances, God looks at the heart. (1 Samuel 16:1-13).

❦

Each of us has two selves – an outer self and an inner self. The outer self could be called the shell, and the inner self the kernel.

Most of us get our self-worth from what others think of us. Hence, in our thirst for approval, acceptance, and status, we may promote the outer self at the expense of the inner self. If we do, we will end up with the appearance rather than the reality. Then our life will be a pretence, and deep down we will know it.

We cannot achieve either happiness or holiness as long as we pretend to be what we are not. The moment we try to be what we are not, we become a fictitious personality. Our priority must be to get the inner self right. It is the source of who we are, what we can be, and what we have to give. If we take care of the inner self, the outward self will take care of itself. There is an axiom which says: As in the inner, so in the outer.

❧

Jesus was able to see beneath the appearance to the inner person. And to him it was the inner person that mattered. This brought him into conflict with the Scribes and Pharisees.

He wasn't taken in by their pious exterior. Piety is no substitute for goodness. He had some hard things to say about them. Perhaps the hardest thing he said was: 'You are like whitewashed tombs that look handsome on the outside, but inside are full of the dead and every kind of corruption. In the same way, from the outside you look upright, but inside you are full of hypocrisy and lawlessness' (Matthew 23:27-28). Strong stuff!

But the chief fault he found in them was that they lacked charity. For all their piety, they were both cold-hearted and hard-hearted individuals. If one's heart is cold and hard, how can one be virtuous? He also made a stinging indictment of their worship when he said: 'You honour God with your lips, but your hearts are far from him' (Matthew 15:8).

He made it clear that his disciples would have to do better. To them he said, 'If your virtue goes no deeper than that of the Scribes and Pharisees, you will never enter the kingdom of heaven' (Matthew 5:20). Virtue is not exterior demeanour or conformity to social manners. Genuine virtue is interior, that is, rooted in conviction and desire. It is an expression of the heart and the soul.

❧

The thing to aim at, then, is goodness of heart. Those who achieve goodness of heart do not have to advertise it or even want to. They know with a quiet certainty that they have something which no one can take from them, something which makes them feel worthwhile, no matter what others may think of them. They have self-esteem and self-respect.

When all is said and done it is the heart that matters. A person is what the heart is. But only God can make the heart what it is meant to be. And only God can see what the heart is like. That is why only God can truly judge people. The person who is falsely accused will take comfort from this.

Our chief concern, then, must be to get the heart right. If the heart is right, then our deeds will be true and genuine. They will flow from what we are, as naturally as good fruit from a good tree.

## Purifying the Heart

TODAY there is great emphasis on cleanness of body, but little or no emphasis on cleanness of mind and heart. When one considers all the advertisements for soaps, washing powders, and perfumes, one is left with the impression that hygiene is more important than morality. The problem is not a new one. Jesus himself encountered it, and among people who should have known better.

❦

One day a Pharisee invited Jesus and his disciples to his house for a meal. Among the guests were several other Pharisees. The latter were shocked when Jesus and his friends sat down to eat without washing their hands. The Pharisees never sat down to a meal without washing their hands from the elbows down. And if they happened to have come in from the market-place, where they might have touched something or someone unclean, they not only washed their hands, but their whole bodies. In their eyes, not to do so was not just bad hygiene, but made a person unclean in the eyes of God.

That is why they were shocked when Jesus and his friends sat down to eat just as they were. So they confronted him: 'Why do your disciples eat without washing their hands?' they asked.

To which Jesus replied, 'Alas for you, Scribes and Pharisees. You hypocrites! You clean the outside of cup and dish and leave the inside full of corruption. Clean the inside of cup and dish and the outside will become clean as well.'

He went on to say, 'There is nothing that goes into people from the outside, that can make them unclean. The only thing that can make people unclean is what comes out of them, what comes out of the heart. It is from inside people that evil springs. From there come things like robbery, murder, adultery, greed, perjury, slander, and so on. And these are the things that make a person unclean in the sight of God.' (Mark 7:1-23).

❦

The problem with the Pharisees was that they saw evil as something entirely outside themselves. But Jesus said that the source of evil is within us. It has its roots in the heart. We can't guard ourselves from it through separation from others. All those horrible things he lists, and which we read about in the newspapers every day – fornication, theft, murder, adultery, greed, malice, deceit, indecency, envy, slander, pride, and so on – all these things start inside a person. These are the things which make a person unclean in the eyes of God.

This is a very disturbing truth, and one we ignore at our own peril. Yet there is a kind of freedom in knowing and accepting it.

Corruption of heart is the worst kind of badness – it is to be bad at the core. Goodness of heart is the best kind of goodness – it is to be good at the core.

So what must we do? We must purify the source. The heart is the source. It is the well-spring from which our thoughts, desires, words, and deeds flow. We must guard it against the things that pollute it, things such as pride, anger, hate, lust, greed, envy, jealousy, spite. If the heart is clean, then all that flows from it will be clean, like water flowing from an unpolluted spring.

How does one purify the heart? By focusing on love. Love purifies the heart. The heart is holy ground. On this holy ground we will see and meet God. 'Blessed are the pure in heart: they shall see God' (Matthew 5:8).

❦

We might make our own the prayer of St Thomas Aquinas:

> Give me, O Lord, an ever-watchful heart, which no subtle speculation may lure from Thee.
> Give me a noble heart, which no unworthy affection can draw downwards to the earth.
> Give me an upright heart, which no insincere intention can warp.
> Give me a firm heart, which no tribulation can crush or quell.
> Give me a free heart, which no perverted affection can claim for its own.

## Seeing with the Heart

SIGHT is a marvellous gift. However, just because we have good eyesight doesn't mean that we see well. There are many things that prevent us from seeing well.

Poor observation means poor seeing. If we don't look we won't see. But it is possible to look and still not see. To see well we have to pay attention.

We are blinded by familiarity. We no longer see what is around us every day. Here children can teach us a lesson because their vision is fresh and clear. This is so because they are seeing everything for the first time. 'If the stars should come out only one night in a thousand years, how people would believe and adore, and preserve for the future generations the remembrance of the city of God which had been shown to them' (Ralph Waldo Emerson).

Often we have eyes only for the extraordinary, and fail to see the wonder of the ordinary. 'The fool wonders at the unusual; the wise person wonders at the usual' (Emerson).

Personal dispositions limit our seeing. For instance, if we are absorbed in ourselves, we simply won't see what is going on around us. The same thing happens when we are in a hurry, or when we are sad, or troubled, or worried. When we are prejudiced, or angry, or bitter, or in pain, our vision is distorted, and we don't see things as they really are. It is said that we see things not as *they* are but as *we* are.

And we must remember that it is not with the eyes only that we see. In fact, to see with the eyes only is to be no better than a camera. There are other ways of 'seeing'. We 'see' with the mind, with the imagination, and with the heart. But here again the question is: how well do we see? A narrow mind, an impoverished imagination, and a small heart, result in poor seeing.

Seeing with the mind could be called *insight*. Here we are talking about the gift of perception. Some people are so perceptive that they are able to see deeply into things, and thus arrive at more valid conclusions.

Seeing with imagination could be called *vision*. It is imagination that enables some people to see where others are blind. People with imagination do not see the same things, nor do they think the same thoughts, as those with no imagination. One day a man came upon Michelangelo as he was chipping away with his chisel at a block of marble, and asked him what he was doing. 'I'm releasing the angel imprisoned in this marble,' he replied.

Seeing with the heart could be called understanding. But it goes deeper than that. It is to see *with compassion*. One person can look at a beggar and feel nothing for him, because he sees him with the eyes only. Another person can look at the same beggar and feel compassion for him, because he sees him with the eyes *and* with the heart.

❦

Jesus was very concerned with the issue of seeing. He was saddened by the blindness he found among his contemporaries: 'They have eyes but do not see' (Mark 4:11). He declared that his mission was 'to open the eyes of the blind' (Luke 4:18). He didn't mean opening people's physical eyes only. To understand how we are meant to see we have to look at him. He is the model for us.

It is clear from the Gospels that Jesus was a keen observer. But he was not a detached observer. What he saw evoked admiration, pity, and at times anger in him.

He had a deep insight into life and into people. We can tell this from his teaching in general and from his parables in particular.

He also had a vivid imagination. His language was littered with striking images and colourful metaphors. The Sermon on the Mount is a good illustration of this.

Furthermore, he had the vision of an artist. For him the world was littered with signs of the Kingdom of God. It wasn't that he didn't see the ugly side of life. He did. He saw the falsity, the cunning, the greed, the cruelty, and the evil. Yet, beneath all of this clutter, disfigurement, and sin, he saw the human being and the child of God.

The Bible is full of little 'background' people. So too is life. They are like stars that never shine. Jesus had an eye for such people. He went out of his way to seek out the lost, the little, the unrecognised, the forgotten, and brought them out of the shadows and into the light.

He looked beneath the surface of people's lives. He saw their wounds and sorrows, their scars and handicaps, their fears, hopes, and longings. He saw how much goodness lies deep within the scarred and disfigured, needing only a word or a touch to release it. There are many examples of this in the Gospels.

Others looked at the leper with disgust, because all they saw was a rotting body. Jesus looked at the leper, and saw a lonely human being, a child of God crying out for the balm of acceptance and healing. (Mark 1:40-45).

The Pharisees looked at sinners with eyes full of condemnation, because all they saw was their vices. Jesus looked at sinners, and saw wounded children of God who could be saints. (Mark 2:15-17).

Some looked at Nathanael sitting under the fig tree, but saw nothing special in him. Jesus looked at Nathanael, and saw a true Israelite, a man incapable of falsity. (John 1:47).

Some looked at Matthew sitting on the steps of the customs house, and saw an idler. Jesus looked at Matthew, and saw a man waiting for a call. (Matthew 9:9).

Some looked at the rich tax collector Zacchaeus perched on the sycamore tree, and saw a scoundrel who deserved to be punished. Jesus looked at Zacchaeus, and saw a man ripe for conversion, a man whose heart was like a bud waiting for the sun. (Luke 19:1-10).

The official teachers looked at the ordinary people, and saw sinners, ignorant of the Law of God. Jesus looked at them, saw sheep without a shepherd, and began to care for them. (Mark 6:34).

Some looked at the widow going into the Temple, and all they saw was a miserable woman making a pathetic offering. Jesus looked at the widow, and saw a poor woman making an heroic offering because she gave all she had. (Mark 12:41-44).

Some looked at the thief on the cross, and saw a criminal getting what he deserved. Jesus looked at the thief, and saw a man longing for Paradise. (Luke 23:39-43).

❦

Jesus saw well. He saw with the eyes, with the mind, and with the imagination. But what set him apart was his ability to see with the heart to a degree unequalled by anyone else.

This explains why, in the beautiful words of Oscar Wilde, 'Jesus understood the leprosy of the leper, the darkness of the blind, the fierce misery of those who live for pleasure, the strange poverty of the rich, the thirst that can lead people to drink from muddy waters. He penetrated the outward shell of things and understood that whatever happens to another happens to oneself, and whatever happens to oneself happens to another.'

Seeing with the heart is the most important kind of seeing of all, because, as the Little Prince said, 'It is only with the heart that one can see rightly. What is essential is invisible to the eye' (Antoine de Saint Exupery).

## Giving with the Heart

I KNOW of a man who made a substantial donation to his church. He gave it directly to the parish priest, who received it gratefully. Because of work commitments, the man had to go to church elsewhere for a few months. When he arrived back in his parish and met the parish priest after Sunday Mass, he was expecting an especially warm greeting. Alas, it didn't happen. The priest greeted him alright, but didn't seem to recognise him. The man was very hurt. What hurt him was not the loss of the money but the lack of recognition. How hard it is to give without expecting something in return.

Giving is at the heart of the Gospel. It is of the very essence of Christianity. It is through giving that the heart remains open and one becomes a loving person. But it has to be the genuine article. There is a marvellous example of the genuine article in the Gospel, and we have this on the authority of Jesus himself.

❧

One day Jesus sat down on the steps near one of the gates of the Temple in Jerusalem. As he sat there he watched visitors to the Temple putting money into a collection box that stood nearby. He noticed that some rich people made large offerings. Then a poor widow came along, and put in two small coins, the equivalent of a cent. On seeing this he called his disciples to him and said, 'I tell you, that widow put in more than any of the others.'

'How could that be?' they asked him.

'The others gave from what they had left over. But she, from the little she had, put in everything she possessed.' (Mark 12:41-44).

❧

This kind of giving is very beautiful but also very rare. How much of our giving is the genuine article? I fear that much of it is tainted by self-interest.

There is the gift that we give with reluctance or regret. This is the gift of the hand, but not of the heart.

There is the gift we give merely out of a sense of duty. This is a cold kind of giving.

There is the gift we give only to our friends. There is nothing great about this. Even crooks are good to their friends.

There is the gift we give because we believe the receiver deserves our gift. This is a judgmental kind of giving.

There is the gift we give simply because of the good feeling we derive from the exercise. This is really self-giving.

There is the gift we give to win the praise and esteem of others. This kind of giving inflates the ego. One can make an idol of oneself through giving. Jesus said, 'When you give alms, don't let your left hand know what your right hand is doing' (Matthew 6:3).

There is the gift that takes the form of a bribe. This doesn't deserve to be called giving. Here, corruption is as much in the giver as in the receiver.

Then, does not much of our giving consist of the giving of left-overs? It is possible to acquire a reputation for generosity by bestowing what costs us nothing. The test of a gift is not what it amounts to in itself, but what its loss means to us. The truest kind of giving is when the gift is as desperately needed by us as by the receiver. Then our gift becomes *a sacrifice*. This was why the offering of the widow drew the praise of Jesus.

❦

There are people who give but only on condition that they receive something in return, and receive it immediately.

There are people who give on condition that they receive something in return, later on and with a handsome profit. This kind of giving is an investment.

But then there are people who give without expecting anything in return, now or ever. They give out of the sheer goodness of their hearts. Giving has become so natural to them that often they don't even know they are giving. In them we see a reflection of God, who lets his sun shine and his rain fall on all of his children, deserving and undeserving.

Some givers are impoverished as they give. Even when giving a small gift, they experience a sense of loss. Why? Because they give grudgingly. But others are enriched as they give. Their hearts are enlarged. Even when giving a large gift, they experience no sense of loss. Why? Because they give joyfully.

Deeds and gifts don't have to be big. Small deeds and small gifts are very important. They may not look much, but they create a friendly atmosphere. Small flowers give off little scent on their own, but put a bunch of them together, and they can fill a room with fragrance. The dawn chorus results from the singing of many little birds. 'Small among the winged creatures is the bee but her produce is the sweetest of the sweet' (Sirach 11:2-3).

Jesus says that anyone who gives one of his disciples even a cup of cold water will be rewarded (Matthew 10: 42). The 'cup of cold water' is a symbol of the small, kind deed. A small deed can bring great comfort to a person provided it has a certain quality. That quality is warmth. All deeds that come from the heart have that quality.

❦

Giving requires that we be sensitive to the receiver. We have to be careful lest in giving it is our own needs that we are meeting.

This is especially important when the receiver is a poor person. We have to be careful lest we reduce the receiver to a state of dependency. Dependency is a pathetic condition. Where there is dependency, there is no development and no growth. There is only stagnation. We have to find a way of giving that doesn't erode the pride and self-respect of the receiver.

In the final analysis, it is not so much a question of giving *things* but of giving of *ourselves,* of our time, our energy, and our talents. 'You give but little when you give of your possessions. It is when you give of yourself that you truly give' (Kahlil Gibran).

There is a striking German proverb which says: 'Birds of prey don't sing.' A bird of prey is essentially a taker, preying on others for its food. I think what the proverb is saying is that there is no joy in taking. But there is great joy in giving.

The vessel with which we give to others is the vessel with which we receive from God. If we are generous towards others, God will see to it that the blessings we bestow will be returned to us, a full measure, pressed down, shaken together, and running over. (Luke 6:38).

## Receiving with the Heart

WE HAVE seen how important it is to be able to give. But it is also important to be able to receive. Even Jesus needed to receive. Shortly before his death he went to Bethany where two sisters, Martha and Mary, gave a dinner in his honour. During dinner Mary produced a jar of very expensive ointment and anointed his feet with it. The perfume was so strong that its scent filled the whole house.

It was a wonderful gesture on Mary's part. But one of the guests didn't see it like that. That was Judas. He complained that it was a waste of money. He said that the perfume should have been sold and the money given to the poor.

A noble sentiment, if he meant it. But he didn't mean it. John tells us that Judas wasn't thinking of the poor but of himself. He was in charge of their funds, and used to help himself to the contributions they got from the people.

Nevertheless, we know Jesus' concern for the poor. Therefore, we would have expected him to agree with Judas, and to call a halt to Mary's extravaganza, or at least to politely refuse it. But he did neither. He accepted Mary's gift, and said to Judas, 'Leave her alone. You have the poor with you always. But I won't be with you always.' (John 12:1-8).

❦

Here Jesus gives us a lesson in how to receive. In spite of the extravagant amount of perfume Mary used, her gesture was in itself a small one. It was just a gesture of gratitude to the man who had raised her brother, Lazarus, from the dead. But it came from her heart. That is why it meant so much to Jesus.

Surrounded by people who always wanted things from him, and by the hostility of those who were plotting his death, it was as welcome as a drink of cold water is to a desert traveller. Besides, for him it took on another and greater significance. He knew his death was near. The Jews always put perfume on the bodies of their dead. Thus, without realising it, Mary had anointed his body for burial.

❦

There are generous people who are very poor at receiving. It is almost impossible to give them anything, or to do them a favour. They are reluctant to ask anyone for help, but always ready to offer help themselves. They may be surrounded by a lot of love, but it is a fountain from which they are unable to drink. Why is this?

It may be that they simply are not aware of their own need.

It may be that they are aware of their need, but hide it for fear of appearing inadequate. People are taught not to admit to being weak. The chief thing is to be strong, and not to be afraid.

It may be that they can't bear being indebted to others. It is too big a blow to their ego. They hate to receive benefits because it makes them feel inferior. But they love to bestow benefits because it makes them feel superior.

It may be that deep down they feel unworthy. They just don't understand undeserved love. They feel they have to prove themselves worthy of love. This makes it difficult for them to ask for help or to receive a gift.

Whatever the reason, it is nothing short of tragic not to be able to receive. There is no such thing as a totally self-sufficient individual. We are remarkably dependent on one another. Other people nourish and sustain us in a hundred different ways.

So what must we do? We must drop our defences, and admit to being the vulnerable and needy human beings that we really are. We have to humble ourselves. True humility doesn't mean demeaning ourselves; it means opening our heart. An open heart

enables us to soak in the kindnesses of others as the parched earth
soaks in the rain. We should adopt the same attitude towards the
blessings of God. The greatest thing we can give to God is a
receptive heart.

❦

Those who recognise their need to receive, and who receive with
graciousness, will be able to give all the better. In fact, it is only
those who know how to receive who know how to give. It takes a
good person to receive a gift well. There is even a way of giving by
receiving. When we receive with graciousness we do wonders for
the giver. We give the giver a chance to love and to enter the world
of sharing.

Giving and receiving are both graced activities. But there has to
be a balance between them. Jesus teaches us not only how to give
but also how to receive. When we give cheerfully, and receive
gratefully, everyone is blessed.

Saint John tells us that the scent of Mary's perfume filled the
entire house. By including the story in his Gospel, he has made it
possible for the fragrance of Mary's deed to fill the entire world.

## Working with the Heart

A HUGE amount of our lives is taken up with work. The nature
of that work is important. But even more important is the
attitude we bring to it. Two people can be doing the exact same
work but bring contrasting attitudes to it, with the result that for
one the work is a blessing, and for the other it is a curse.

❦

Jesus gave an example of this. It concerned two shepherds. The
first he called a 'hireling'; the second he called a 'good shepherd'.
The hireling doesn't really care about the sheep. As soon as he sees
a wolf coming he runs away, and leaves the sheep at the mercy of
the wolf. The good shepherd really cares about the sheep. He is

prepared to lay down his life to defend them from the wolf. (John 10:11-15).

❦

Here we have two people engaged in the exact same work. But what contrasting attitudes they bring to it. One is apathetic and uncaring; the other is dedicated and caring. How do we account for the difference between them? It comes down to a question of motivation.

The hireling is poorly motivated. He is poorly motivated because his heart is not in his work. He is just going through the motions. For him minding the sheep is just a job. He does it, not because he wants to, but because he has to. He doesn't care about the quality of his work. All he cares about is his wages.

The good shepherd, on the other hand, is highly motivated. He is highly motivated because his heart is in the work. For him minding the sheep is not just a job. It is his life. He does it, not because he has to, but because he wants to. For him shepherding is a labour of love.

In one sense this makes it harder for him, because he puts more of himself into it. But in another sense it makes it a lot easier, because it enables him to bring all his energies and talents to it. The easiest actions are those that flow from love. They are like water gushing from a mountain spring.

The hireling is to be pitied. His *work* suffers. And so does *he*. His work suffers because he gives only a part of himself to it. He suffers because something corrosive happens to the soul of the one who stops caring about the quality of his work. The hireling may have an easier life, but he derives no satisfaction from his work. The satisfaction is proportionate to the effort. One gets out of something only what one puts into it.

The good shepherd is to be envied. His *work* prospers. And so does *he*. His work prospers because he puts his entire self, mind, body and soul, into it. He prospers because the work brings out the best in him. Besides, it saves him from half-heartedness, and from the tragedy of only half-living his life. It is not enough to employ people's hands. Their minds and hearts must work also.

❧

Most of us are hirelings because we do not work for ourselves. But that doesn't mean that we have to have the mentality of the hireling. We can still bring the attitude of the good shepherd to our work.

But those who have something in their lives that they are passionate about are very fortunate. It doesn't have to be something big. It can be something small, something useful. Even if at times it proves a crucifixion, the pride they feel, and the satisfaction they derive from doing it well, more than compensates them for any pain. We must never equate an easy life with a happy life.

The painter, Vincent van Gogh, agonised over what he wanted to do with his life. Eventually he discovered that he wanted to be a painter. It was the defining moment in his life. Later he wrote: 'I often feel that I am as rich as Croesus, not in money, but rich because I have found my work. In that work I have something to which I can devote myself heart and soul, and which gives meaning and inspiration to my life.' (*The Letters of Vincent Van Gogh*)

It wasn't that his life suddenly became rosy. The opposite would be nearer the truth. Yet he was able to say: 'If at times I feel rising within me the desire for a life of ease, I go back fondly to a life of hardship, convinced that I learn more from it. This is not the road on which one perishes. On the contrary, this is a powerful stream that will bear me safely to port.'

Of himself Jesus said: 'I am the good shepherd; I know my own and my own know me. I lay down my life for my sheep' (John 10:14-15). That says it all. And in his case it was not just so many words. He meant what he said. He did give his life for his sheep.

## Caring for the Heart

A POND must have an inlet and an outlet. If there is no inlet, the pond will dry up. If there is no outlet, it will turn into a swamp.

Similarly we need a balance between input and output in our lives. In what follows the emphasis is on input.

We live in an increasingly frenetic and competitive society. It is easy to get so caught up in work that we haven't a minute for ourselves. This can result in restless and impoverished lives. Here generous people are more at risk than selfish people. The answer lies in taking time out to care for ourselves. Only by paying careful attention to our own physical, emotional, and spiritual needs can we remain joyful givers. Even Jesus needed to take time out for himself.

❧

In his Gospel, St Mark shows Jesus constantly surrounded by people. So many wanted to touch him that at times he was in danger of being crushed (3:9). So many were clamouring for his attention that at times he couldn't even have a meal (3:20). How did he cope with all of this pressure? He went off to quiet places to rest and to pray. To take two examples.

One Sabbath day, early in his public ministry, he preached at the local synagogue where he also cured a sick man. Afterwards he retired to Peter's house for refreshments. But he didn't get much peace there either. Peter's mother-in-law was sick and he attended to her. But it was after sundown, when the Sabbath officially ended, that the real trouble began. People came crowding round the door, bringing with them all those who were suffering from diseases of one kind or another. He cured many of them. It must have been all hours by the time he got to bed. Yet he rose early next morning, and went off to a lonely place to pray (1:32-35).

We find a similar thing after the miracle of the loaves and fishes. Having dismissed the people and sent the apostles back across the lake, alone at last, he went into the hills to pray (6:46).

These two examples are not exceptions. This was his customary practice. He knew how to combine action and contemplation. In the midst of the hectic activity which filled his days, he found time to withdraw by himself to lonely places.

What did the lonely place do for him? It enabled him to get some much needed rest. It helped him to keep focused on his mission. But, above all, it gave him time to pray. It was prayer that enabled him to maintain and foster the most important thing in his life – his relationship with his heavenly Father. That relationship was the ground beneath his feet all life long and the secret of his successful ministry.

ꙮ

We too need to withdraw from our activities from time to time in order to care for ourselves. Yet how many of us manage to do this on a regular basis? Even though we may be convinced of its benefits, we don't find it an easy thing to do. Why is this?

One reason is: we don't know how to cope with idleness and stillness. To withdraw means to stop our activity. But as soon as we stop our activity, we begin to feel empty, perhaps even useless. Most of us get our sense of self-worth from doing. Our value as persons depends on our usefulness. Hence the compulsion to keep busy. Activity can become a disease.

Another reason is: we are afraid of self-examination. Over-work can be a flight from self. To withdraw is to put ourselves in for some serious self-examination. Self-examination is something few of us find easy but which can be enormously beneficial. Merely to reflect on the transience of our lives and our undertakings, is a kind of purification and a test as well.

A third reason is: we can't cope with loneliness. Loneliness can be very painful. What makes loneliness so painful is not the absence of people – one can be lonely in a crowd – but the emptiness we feel. Therefore, we fill the void with endless distractions. Work can be a defence against loneliness.

But loneliness is inescapable. We all have a life of our own which cannot be shared with anyone. The fact that we are separate individuals will always involve a certain degree of loneliness. However, it is possible to be alone without being lonely. This is what solitude is about. Solitude is different from loneliness. Loneliness is the pain of being alone. Solitude is the joy of being alone. Without solitude it is very difficult to have an inner life.

If we knew how to withdraw, *we* would benefit. And *our work* would benefit. We would benefit because just as we can lose ourselves in work, we can also find ourselves in work. Our work would benefit because the quiet time would enable us to draw ourselves together, so that we are able to work from our purest and deepest springs.

A quiet space is absolutely necessary in order to maintain our connection with God. We are not taking the spiritual life seriously if we do not set aside some time to be with God. Each day we should try, if only for a short while, to withdraw to a quiet place in order to seek the face of God. Just to sit in such a place is a good thing. In it we not only find God but ourselves too. In the quiet and stillness of God's presence, our projects lose their power over us, and we experience our true worth, which consists not in doing but in being.

❦

It is the heart that needs the quiet place most, and it is the heart that benefits most from it. We have to care for the heart as we would care for a wood fire. The quiet place enables us to calm the restless heart, to rest the weary heart, to replenish the empty heart, to purify the sullied heart, to re-focus the scattered heart, and to heal the wounded heart. There is a saying: when the heart gets sick, everything gets sick. The opposite is also true: when the heart gets well, everything gets well.

# Healing the Wounds of the Heart

THE American poet, Henry Wadsworth Longfellow, said: 'If we could read the secret history of our enemies we should find in each person's life sorrow and suffering enough to disarm all hostility.' How true. It's amazing how when you know a person's story, or even just a part of it, your attitude towards that person changes.

Once on Ash Wednesday I went to administer blessed ashes to the inmates of a prison. I knew that the young men who were locked up there had been convicted of very serious crimes. Giving them the ashes gave me an opportunity to look at their faces.

The first thing that struck me was the deep sadness that was etched on their faces. The second thing was the fact that there was scarcely one of them that didn't carry a scar. I was conscious of the fact that I was seeing only the surface; a face conceals more than it reveals. God alone knew how wounded these young men were at heart. Yes, they had hurt others. But they were deeply wounded themselves. When I realised this I was filled with compassion for them.

In one way or another all of us are wounded. Many people carry wounds in their bodies. But the part of us that is most deeply wounded is the heart. The heart is wounded by such things as disappointment, ingratitude, grief, rejection, and betrayal. Betrayal is like a dagger through the heart. A wounded body will heal naturally, but not a wounded heart. The human heart is healed only by the presence of another human being who understands human pain.

❦

On Easter Sunday evening the apostles were gathered in the upper room behind locked doors. The room was full of bitter-sweet memories for them. It was here the Master had washed their feet and celebrated the Last Supper with them. But it was here too that they had sworn loyalty to him, a loyalty which didn't even see the night through.

The apostles were wounded men. They were wounded, not in body, but in heart and in spirit. They were wounded individually by fear, doubt, guilt, grief and despair. And they were wounded collectively because one of their number, Judas, had killed himself. Like all people in pain, they had erected a barrier around themselves.

Jesus knew how they were feeling. In one bold move he broke through the barrier, and stood among them. He didn't scold them for failing him. Instead, he greeted them with the lovely words, 'Peace be with you.' He repeated those words to make sure they got the message. In receiving his peace, they received his forgiveness.

Then what did he do? He showed them his own wounds. Why? So that they could recognise him as the same Jesus who had been crucified. There is one feature which is common to all the resurrection stories: the risen Jesus is not immediately recognisable. This is a way of making the point that resurrection is not a return to earthly life as before. Jesus has risen to a new life beyond death, a life with God. He is the same person, yet changed.

Having convinced them that it really was he, he said to them, 'As the Father sent me, so I am sending you. Receive the Holy Spirit. If you forgive anyone's sins, they are forgiven.' From these words they understood that he was sending them out as ministers of God's forgiveness to others. (John 20:19-23).

❦

Jesus didn't insulate himself against human pain. On the contrary, he made himself totally vulnerable by taking to himself our fragile, mortal humanity. And he paid the price. But we would have expected his risen body to be without blemish. Yet it still bore the marks of our violent world.

He didn't hide his wounds. For him they were not things to be ashamed of. They were more like badges of honour. They were the proof of his love. They were eloquent witnesses to how costly real love can be. Wounds are the greatest form of witness.

St Paul didn't hide his wounds either. He said, 'The marks on my body are those of Christ' (Galatians 6:17). He was probably referring to the scars left on his body by hardship, illness, flogging, stoning, and so on. His service of Christ had been a costly one. He had the wounds to prove it.

Forty years after leaving Auschwitz, the Italian writer, Primo Levi, still bore on his arm the tattoo with the number he got while there. When people asked him why he didn't have it erased he replied, 'Why should I? There are not many of us left in the world to bear witness.'

❦

The way of Jesus is the way of love. And the way of love is the way of the cross. But there is nothing terrible about suffering a little if it teaches us to love. If we suffer in the cause of love, the wounds we bear will be honourable wounds. They will mark us out as true disciples of Jesus.

That doesn't mean we should not seek to be healed of our wounds. We should. And we should not settle for a superficial healing. We should aim at nothing less than deep healing. Sometimes we are tempted to hide our wounds. For healing to happen, we have to show our wounds to someone, and to re-open them if necessary.

But the question that is always asked is: why re-open old wounds? The short answer is: because they are badly closed. Unless we cure the infection, the wound will open of itself. When we have the courage to open our hurt self, and to deal with our repressed pain, we begin to heal.

Jesus didn't glorify suffering. Nor was he sentimental about it. But the fact that he could and did suffer is a great consolation to us. It means that he understands our pain. Suffering is a lonely condition. It can destroy a person. There are wounds from which the heart may never heal. 'Too long a sacrifice can make a stone of the heart' (W. B. Yeats). Some people allow suffering to take control of their lives with the result that they become perpetual victims.

Suffering can benefit us. The value of suffering does not lie in the pain of it, but in what we make of it. Suffering can enable us to tap rich sources of strength within ourselves. In can also soften our hardened hearts and enable us to empathise with other sufferers.

It is true that it may leave us a little fragile. But this fragility will make us gentler and more sensitive in dealing with the wounds of others. When we empathise with other sufferers we too benefit. In the simple act of showing sympathy for others there is healing.

❦

The heart of one person holds inexhaustible sources of life for the heart of another. But for this to happen the heart must be right. Alas, the heart is not always right. It is often empty. It is often cold and unwelcoming. It is often hard and unyielding. It is often weighed down with worry. It is often lonely. It is often in darkness. It is often wounded. And it is sometimes broken. We have to heal the wounds of the heart in order to be able to bear the fruits of love. God doesn't want our suffering. God wants our love.

# The Heart's Memory

THERE is an insightful little story which goes like this. Once a traveller came upon a barn where the devil stored seed which he planned to sow in the hearts of people. There were bags of seeds variously marked 'Hatred', 'Fear', 'Doubt', 'Despair', 'Unforgiveness', 'Pride', and so on.

The devil appeared and struck up a conversation with the traveller. He gleefully told him how easily the seeds he sowed sprouted in the hearts of men and women.

'Are there any hearts in which these seeds will not sprout?' the traveller asked.

A melancholy look appeared on the devil's face. 'These seeds will not sprout in the heart of a grateful and joyful person,' he confessed.

❦

On the way up to Jerusalem Jesus travelled along the border between Samaria and Galilee. As he was entering a village, ten lepers came to meet him. They stood some way off and called to him, 'Jesus! Master! Take pity on us.' When he saw them he said, 'Go and show yourselves to the priests.' (The priests were the only people who could officially authenticate their cure, and thus open the way for them to return to society).

Now as they were going away they were cured. Finding himself cured, one of them turned back praising God at the top of his voice and threw himself at the feet of Jesus and thanked him. The man was a Samaritan. (The implication is that the others were Jews).

This caused Jesus to say, 'Were not all ten made clean? The other nine, where are they? It seems that no one has come back to give praise to God, except this foreigner.' And he said to the man, 'Stand up and go on your way. Your faith has saved you.' (Luke 17:11-19).

❦

In ridding them of leprosy Jesus had done an enormous thing for those ten people. The very least they might have done was to come back and say 'thanks'. Yet nine of them failed to do even that. It is only the dumb animals who cannot say thanks.

What does this tell us about the nine? It suggests that they returned home with bitterness in their hearts. This means that they were cured in body only. Their leprosy was gone, but nothing else about them had changed. People have been known to return from close brushes with death to lives of superficiality and mediocrity, and even to lives of crime and sin. They learn nothing from their pain.

The one man who did come back to thank Jesus was a Samaritan, that is, an outsider. But that's how it often is. The outsider sees everything as a gift; the insider takes everything for granted. The Samaritan just *had* to express his thanks. What does this tell us about him? It suggests that he was cured not only physically but also spiritually. Of the ten, he was the only one who was brought closer to God through his illness.

It is hard not to be affected by ingratitude. Ingratitude can make a kind person turn bitter. There is no suggestion that Jesus was affected by the ingratitude of the nine. While it is true that he demanded gratitude, he didn't demand it for himself. What he said was, 'Has no one come back to give praise *to God* except this foreigner.' From this it is clear that he wasn't thinking of himself but of the lepers. If anyone finds another person ungrateful, it is not the other person's happiness he is seeking, but his own.

❦

Gratitude is something that ought to come naturally to us. Sadly, this is far from being the case. We are better at remembering insults than favours. 'We write in the sand the benefits we receive, but the injuries we write on marble' (Thomas More). And we are better at demanding gratitude than at giving it. The person who is not grateful for small favours will not be grateful for big ones.

It is very important for us to be able to express thanks to those who are good to us. It is good for ourselves in the first place; it forces us to acknowledge the debt we owe to others. And it is good for our benefactors; it makes them feel appreciated.

And it is especially important for us to express thanks to God. God doesn't need our thanks. But we need to thank him. It is a way of acknowledging that we owe everything to him. However, it is easy to be grateful to God for the good things that happen to us, but very difficult to be grateful for the painful things.

We must try to be grateful for all of our lives, the bad as well as the good, the sorrows as well as the joys. When we look back over our lives, we see that the things that hurt us and the things that helped us cannot be separated from each other. We must try to see the guiding hand of a loving God in all that has brought us to where we are now. Not all that happens to us is determined by God's will, but all is encompassed by his love.

❦

Gratitude does wonders for the heart. 'I used to think gratitude a heavy burden for one to carry. Now I know that it is something that makes the heart lighter. The ungrateful person seems to me to be one who walks with feet and heart of lead' (Oscar Wilde).

A grateful heart is a joyful heart. And there is no room in a grateful and joyful heart for bitterness, or for a lot of other things either. Gratitude is the heart's memory. It makes us want to give something back. 'If the only prayer you ever say in your life is "Thank you, Lord," it will be enough' (Meister Eckhart).

## The Sting

ON A bright and sunny morning Ellen set out to deliver flowers to her friend Mary on her birthday. She was in high spirits and sang as she went along. But then, out of the blue, a wasp swooped and stung her in the arm. What had been a sweet journey suddenly turned sour.

Leaving aside the flowers, she sat down by the side of the road to inspect the damage. She had no difficulty in locating the spot in which she had been stung for it felt very sore, had turned red, and was swelling up alarmingly. As she sat there wincing with pain and feeling very sorry for herself, a passer-by stopped.

'What's the matter?' the stranger asked in a kindly voice.

'I've just been stung by a wasp,' Ellen replied.

'I know exactly how you feel. I've often been stung myself,' said the stranger.

'But why did the wasp have to pick on me? I did nothing to provoke him,' said Ellen.

The stranger made no reply. Instead, she took out a jar of ointment and applied some of it to the wound. The ointment had a soothing effect on the wound, and not long afterwards Ellen was on her way again. However, as she went along, she couldn't keep her eyes off the wound. Fortunately the swelling subsided and the pain eased somewhat.

Along the way she met up with other travellers. She insisted on telling them about the wasp sting and even showing them the wound. With every telling, the wasp got more vicious and the wound more serious. Though her confidants could barely make out the wound, they could see that Ellen was very bitter about it. All of them tried to help her.

'Ignore it,' said one.

'Put it behind you,' said a second.

'Treat it as if it never happened,' said a third.

And so it went on. Though her advisers used different expressions, their advice came to the same thing: forget the sting. This sounded like good advice and she grasped at it.

She tried to forget the sting. God knows she tried. However, memory is a strange thing. We forget the things we want to remember, and we remember the things we want to forget. So, no matter how hard she tried, the sting just would not stay forgotten. It kept popping up like a decapitated weed. And every time it popped up she felt a stab of pain.

This might have gone on for the entire journey had she not had the good fortune to meet up with an old and wise friend by the name of Sheila. Naturally she opened her heart to her also.

'Forget the whole thing! Why should you forget it?' asked Sheila.

The question surprised Ellen. She hesitated, then replied, 'Everybody I meet tells me that I should forget it.'

'But it happened,' Sheila insisted gently. 'It's part of the story of your journey. Besides, it's not something to be ashamed of.'

'But the trouble is that every time I remember it, I feel the hurt all over again,' said Ellen.

'It's *how* you remember it that matters,' said Sheila. 'You're on a mission of love, aren't you?'

'Yes.'

'Well then, don't let the sting distract you from that. Above all, don't let its poison diminish your love. Then when you arrive at your friend's house, your gift will be all the more precious because you suffered a wound in delivering it.'

After they parted, Ellen reflected on what her friend had said. She came to see the sting in a new light. With that the bitterness left her, and once again she found herself going along with a light heart and a happy step.

# The Mercy of Fathers

THERE are innumerable stories about love. The following is one of my favourite ones. In it an old man is reminiscing with his son, Willie, about an incident that happened in his youth.

One time, Willie, and it was Christmastime too, and I was a young fellow in Kiltegan, our dog Shep went missing for some days, as dogs in winter will. I was maybe ten or eleven and I loved that Shep, and feared he was gone forever. We had got him as a young dog that had been beaten somewhere, and broken, till he reached our haven, and uncoiled, and learned to bark like a baby learns to laugh, and he shone at his work.

One morning early after a fall of snow I went out to break the ice on the rain-barrel to plash my face, and saw tracks in the snow going up the sloping field, and I was greatly afeared, because there were drops of blood now and then as he went, little smears of it on the clean snow. So I followed him up, sinking here and there in the drifts, and on a piece of field we called the upper garden, because it was flat there and you could see across to Baltinglass and some said even to Shillelagh and the dark woods of Coollattin, I found our dog there with the carcass of a ewe well-eaten, only the hindquarters remaining. I saw my father's blue sign on the wool and knew the worst. For a dog that would kill a sheep would die himself.

So in my innocence I went down to my father and told him, and he instructed me, as was right and proper, to go back up with a rope and lead Shep down so the killing could take place. The loss of a ewe was a disaster. But I loved the dog so sorely, I hesitated when I had the rope tied about him, and at length led him off further up the hill, across the little stand of scrubby pines, and on into the low woods dark with snow and moss. And we went through by a snaking path I knew, till we got to the other side, where there was a simple man living, that made his living from the rabbits, and maybe had need of a watchful dog.

But he wouldn't take a dog that had killed, though he was a tender man enough, and it behoved me to retrace my steps back into the woods, now moving along but slowly, and the dog sort of dragging behind, as if he knew well his misdeed and his fate. And I stopped in the centre of the trees, and do you know my young legs would not go forward, they would not proceed, try as I might, and there I was all that afternoon and night with the dog and the hazels.

How is it that the drear of winter didn't eat my bones and murder me for my foolishness? Love of the dog kept me standing there, as only a child can stand, without moving, thinking, the poor dog whimpering with the cold. About five o'clock I went on, because I heard calling over the hill, here and there, and I could see black figures with lights moving and calling, calling out to me and the dog to come home.

We came down the sloping field with the neighbours about us, them not saying a word, maybe marvelling at me, thinking I had been dead, and the torches and lamps making everything crazy with light, the old crab apple enlarging to the size of the field, its branches wild like arms. Down at last into the yard we came, the dog skulking on the rope just the same as the day he had arrived to us, and my father came out from the house in his big clothes. It was as if I had never seen him before, never looked at him in his entirety, from head to toe. And I knew then that the dog and me were for slaughter.

My feet carried me on to where he stood, immortal you would say in the door. And he put his right hand on the back of my head, and pulled me to him so that my cheek rested against the buckle of his belt. And he raised his face to the brightening sky and praised someone, in a crushed voice, God maybe, for my safety, and stroked my hair. And the dog's crime was never spoken of, but that he lived till he died.

And I would call that the mercy of fathers, when the love that lies in them deeply like the glittering face of a well is betrayed by an emergency, and the child sees at last that he is loved, loved and needed, and not to be lived without.

(Sebastian Barry, *The Steward of Christendom*, London, Reed International, with the permission of the author)

PART FIVE

# *Last Words*

# It Is the Heart That Matters

It is only with the heart that we can see rightly. To see with the eyes only is to be no better than a camera.

It is only with the heart that we can hear rightly. The cry of a needy person may reach our ears, but unless it reaches our heart we will not feel the person's pain, and it is unlikely that we will respond.

It is only with the heart that we can speak rightly. For our words to ring true, they must come from the heart. If they come only from the lips, they will have a hollow sound and will have little effect. They will be like a wind that ruffles the surface of the water but leaves the depth untouched.

It is only with the heart that we can give rightly. If our gift does not come from the heart, it will not ennoble us or enrich the receiver. It is possible to give generously with the hand and still be a miser at heart.

It is only with the heart that we can work rightly. If our heart is in our work, the work becomes a joy and we put our best into it. But if our heart is not in our work, we are working under the severest handicap of all.

It is only with the heart that we can welcome a person rightly. We may open the door of our home to someone, but unless we make room for that person in our heart, he or she will still be a stranger to us.

It is only with the heart that we can forgive rightly. If forgiveness does not come from the heart, it will not bring us peace, nor will it result in a true reconciliation with the other party.

It is only with the heart that we can repent rightly. If our repentance does not reach our heart, it will not lead to a change of life. It will be like decapitating weeds while leaving their roots intact.

It is only with the heart that we can worship God rightly. If our heart is not in our worship, we are no better than an answering machine – our voice is present but we are absent.

It is only with the heart that we can know God rightly. We could know facts about God, and still not know God. Loving is the only way to know God and to share in God's life.

❧

An earnest young man approached a monk and said, 'Tell me what God is like.' 'Do you see the sun?' the monk began. The student raised his eyes towards the sky, but the monk said, 'No, don't look at it or you'll damage your eyes. Instead, hold out your arm and roll up your sleeve.' The student did as he was directed.

'Do you feel the sun?' asked the monk.

'I do,' nodded the student, still mystified.

'You think it is very far away, yet you can feel it on your arm,' said the monk.

'Yes, but what does that have to do with God?' the student asked.

'You want to know what God is like.'

'Yes.'

'Your problem is that you have a cold heart.'

'So what must I do?'

'You must bare your heart to love just as you have bared your arm to the sun. If you do that you will know what God is like.'

❧

When all is said and done it is the heart that matters. To close one's heart is to begin to die. To open one's heart is to begin to live. The world is God's temple. The human heart is his sanctuary.

# Witness of Saints, Poets and Philosophers

Saints, theologians, philosophers, political leaders and writers all have enunciated important truths about the heart. Even though some of these quotations are included in the previous pages, I wanted to bring them together here so that they might bear collective witness to the truth of what I have been saying in a roundabout way in the course of the book.

You made us for yourself, O Lord, and our hearts will never rest until they rest in you. (St Augustine)

If God has not got your heart, he has nothing. (St Thérèse of Lisieux)

Great tranquility of heart is his who cares for neither praise nor blame. (Thomas à Kempis)

Atheism is rather in the lip than in the heart of man.(Francis Bacon)

The heart has its reasons of which reason itself knows nothing. (Blaise Pascal)

We will never believe with a vigorous and unquestioning faith unless God touches our hearts; it is to the heart that the call of God comes. (Blaise Pascal)

Speak to people's hearts, and they suddenly become virtuous. (Ralph Waldo Emerson)

What is true for you in your own private heart, is true for all people. (Ralph Waldo Emerson)

The heart of one person holds inexhaustible sources of life for the heart of another. (Fyodor Dostoevsky)

Nobody has ever measured, not even poets, how much a heart can hold. (Zelda Fitzgerald)

In most hearts there is an empty chamber waiting for a guest. (Nathaniel Hawthorne)

When God measures a person, he puts the tape around the heart instead of the head. (Author unknown)

On the scales of God only the heart has any weight. (Karl Rahner S.J.)

Fear not that your heart might be broken; fear, rather, that it might turn into a stone. (Oscar Wilde)

Too long a sacrifice can make a stone of the heart. (William Butler Yeats)

Love is never lost. If not reciprocated, it will flow back and soften and purify the heart. (Washington Irving)

Hatred towards any human being cannot exist in the same heart as love of God. (William Inge)

Hate is the seed of death in my heart, love is the seed of life. (Thomas Merton)

If you are bitter at heart, sugar in the mouth will not help you. (Jewish proverb)

Home is where the heart is. (Proverb)

It is only with the heart that one can see rightly; what is essential is invisible to the eye. (Antoine de Saint Exupery)

If people are to strive with all their heart, the significance of their striving must be unmistakable. (Antoine de Saint Exupery)

Those who don't know how to weep with their whole heart don't know how to laugh either. (Golda Meir)

Joy in the heart is the surest sign of the presence of God. (Leon Bloy)

Terrible things can happen to a person with an empty heart. (Gerald Vann, O.P.)

If you haven't any charity in your heart, you have the worst kind of heart trouble. (Bob Hope)

My strength is as the strength of ten, because my heart is pure. (Alfred Lord Tennyson)

If seeds in the black earth can turn into such beautiful roses, what might not the heart of man become in its long journey towards the stars? (Gilbert Keith Chesterton)

Do we not all secretly long for more love than reason, more pardon than justice, more impulse than calculation, more heart than head? (Laurens van der Post)

Even in hearts that are overwhelmed by evil, one small bridge-head of good is retained. And in the best of all hearts, there remains an unuprooted small corner of evil. (Alexander Solzhenitsyn)

A compassionate heart can heal almost anything. (Elizabeth Kubler-Ross)

Is there anything more holy than the deep longings of the human heart? (Patrick Kavanagh)